YELLOWSTONE &
GRAND TETON'S
BEST NATURE WALKS

YELLOWSTONE & GRAND TETON'S BEST NATURE WALKS

29 EASY WAYS TO EXPLORE THE PARKS' ECOLOGY

RODDY SCHEER

TIMBER PRESS + PORTLAND, OREGON

To Thomas Moran and William Henry Jackson:
Thanks for helping me see the light.

Frontispiece: Biscuit Basin, toward Mystic Falls

Copyright © 2024 by Roddy Scheer. All rights reserved.

Photo and illustration credits appear on page 250.

Timber Press
Workman Publishing
Hachette Book Group, Inc.
1290 Avenue of the Americas
New York, New York 10104
timberpress.com

Timber Press is an imprint of Workman Publishing, a division of Hachette Book Group, Inc. The Timber Press name and logo are registered trademarks of Hachette Book Group, Inc.

Printed in China on responsibly sourced paper
Text and cover design by Hillary Caudle

The publisher is not responsible for websites (or their content) that are not owned by the publisher.

The Hachette Speakers Bureau provides a wide range of authors for speaking events. To find out more, go to hachettespeakersbureau.com or email HachetteSpeakers@hbgusa.com.

ISBN 978-1-64326-153-9

A catalog record for this book is available from the Library of Congress.

CONTENTS

INTRODUCTION

This book provides an introduction to Yellowstone and Grand Teton national parks through the lens of ecology—the study of the relationships between living organisms and their physical environment. While we all love visiting wild and natural places, it's hard to pick which trails to hike that won't be as crowded but will be scenic, recreational, and educational. Often, when we do discover a hike we like, we find out so little about the inner workings of nature that make a particular place tick. I hope the pages of this book will fill in some of those knowledge gaps for those who care to dig a little deeper into the places they're visiting around Greater Yellowstone.

It was my great pleasure to research this project, driving to all of the featured sites to stop at pullouts and hike the trails—all under two miles round-trip, so anyone can do them—while documenting the ecological relationships I witnessed.

Appreciating the wild nature we can still find at Yellowstone and Grand Teton today is essential to protecting it for future generations, especially in this world where environmental threats are now not just local, but global in nature. The idea of the Best Nature Walks series is to focus on short hikes and even roadside pullouts where anybody can access wondrous natural environments that fit into the bigger regional picture but are also unique in one or more ways. Greater Yellowstone is chock full of alluring landscapes

▲ The foundation for Yellowstone National Park was laid 630,000 years ago when a supervolcano here erupted, ejecting enough ash into the atmosphere to darken skies around the world for 2 years, wiping out untold numbers of species worldwide. Here at ground zero, the volcano collapsed into itself, creating the 30-by 45-mile caldera that now forms the park's approximate border. Over the eons, a host of additional natural phenomena shaped this place into the landscapes we know today, like this one, the Grand Canyon of the Yellowstone.

populated with charismatic fauna and diverse and beautiful flora. Let this book be your guide to a few of these special spots and your springboard to explore further on your own.

Happy trails!

Believe it or not, the Tetons we admire today are relatively young—that's why the peaks are so pointy, jagged, and tall! They formed just 10 million years ago (a wink in time geologically) when two tectonic plates collided, creating a 40-mile uplift along a deep underground fault.

YELLOWSTONE

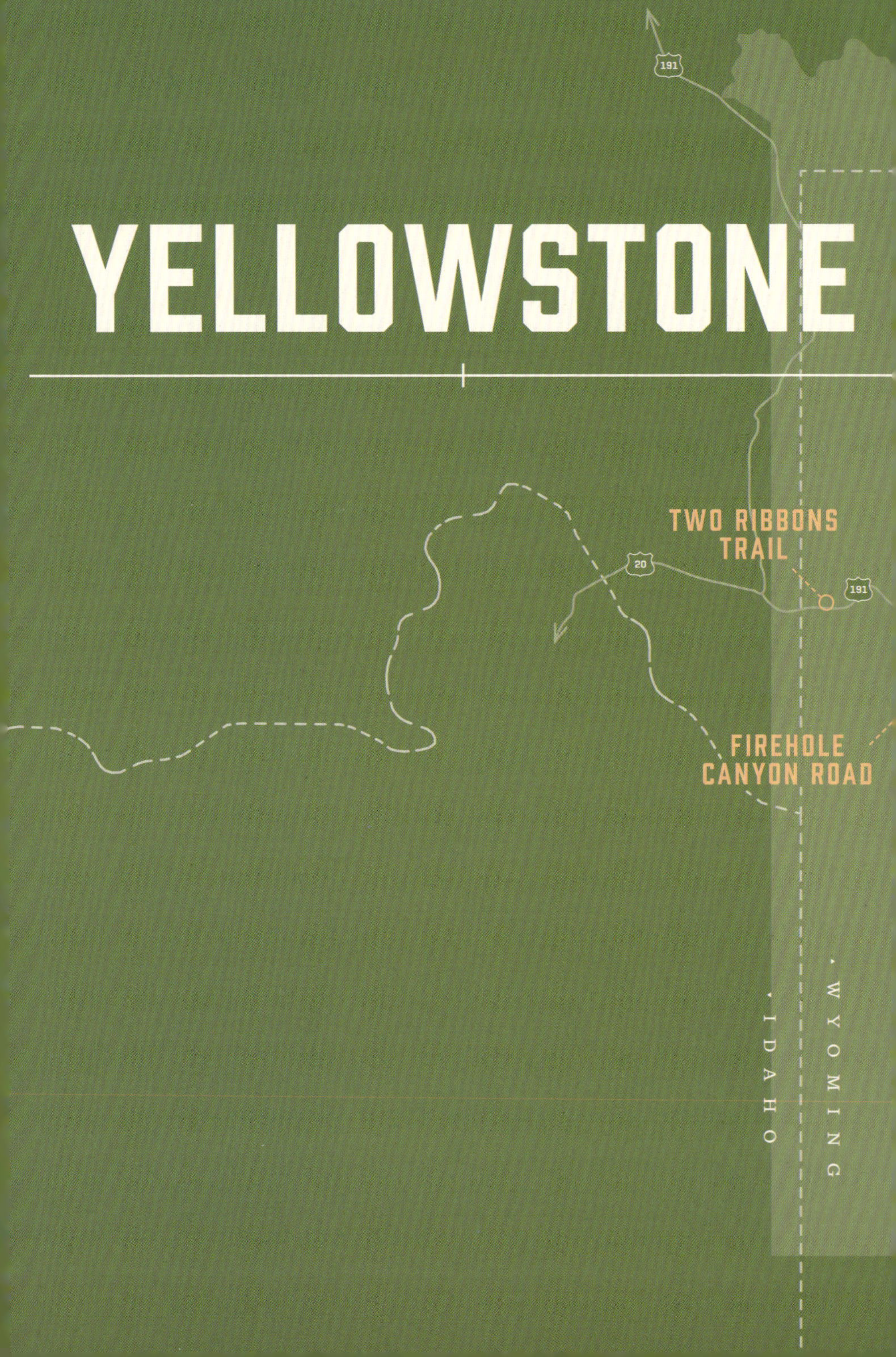

191

TWO RIBBONS
TRAIL

20

191

FIREHOLE
CANYON ROAD

W Y O M I N G

I D A H O

MAMMOTH
HOT SPRINGS

FORCES OF THE
NORTHERN RANGE

• MONTANA

THE
HOODOOS

YELLOWSTONE
RIVER PICNIC
AREA

89

WRAITH
FALLS

PETRIFIED
TREE

212

TROUT
LAKE

89

SHEEPEATER
CLIFF

NORRIS
GEYSER
BASIN

ICE LAKE

LAMAR
VALLEY

ARTIST POINT TO
LILY PAD LAKE

ARTISTS'
PAINTPOTS

HAYDEN VALLEY
MUD VOLCANO

MONUMENT
GEYSER BASIN

191

PELICAN CREEK
NATURE TRAIL

FIREHOLE LAKE
DRIVE

STORM
POINT

BISCUIT BASIN AND
MYSTIC FALLS

Yellowstone
Lake

14

GEYSER HILL AND
OBSERVATION POINT

191

TWO RIBBONS TRAIL

Riparian loop shows lodgepole pine forest's resilience and recovery from wildfire

DIFFICULTY
Easy

LOCATION
West-Central Yellowstone (Madison)

HIKE LENGTH
.75 miles

The Two Ribbons Trail boardwalk cuts through lots of mountain big sagebrush and some mature lodgepole pines on its way to the Madison River.

The two ribbons of this loop along the shallow, fast-moving Madison River traverse two very different forests. If you're entering the park from the west (like most visitors), walking the Two Ribbons Trail is a great soft introduction to Yellowstone. No thermal features here, and wildlife sightings are few and far between—you will see lots of Rocky Mountain lodgepole pines, the park's dominant tree species. One ribbon runs along the riverside, with fewer, more mature trees and sagebrush filling in the gaps. The other features newer growth literally from the ashes (and fallen logs) of wildfires that ravaged much of Yellowstone and Grand Teton national parks in 1988. You'll find the western trailhead by the kiosk at a well-marked pullout and parking area along the north side of US Route 191.

The trail quickly joins a boardwalk that snakes through mature lodgepole pines on its way to the river. You'll see plenty of resilient elder lodgepoles in this beautiful ribbon of mature forest abutting the Madison River, spared by wind and perhaps their proximity to the river during the apocalyptic fires of 1988, unlike the latter section of this boardwalk loop.

LODGEPOLE PINE: THE QUINTESSENTIAL YELLOWSTONE TREE

The lodgepole pine tree thrives at an elevation of 6000 to 8000 feet and withstands harsh conditions and little water, so it's no surprise it dominates the ecology here—some 1.4 million acres of the 2.2 million-acre national park are covered in various stages of lodgepole forest.

In perfect soil conditions with little competition, lodgepole pines achieve heights north of 150 feet, with diameters pushing 30 inches. In Yellowstone,

with its thermally compromised soils and stiff competition, the biggest grow about 80 feet, with diameters maxing out at 16 inches. By age 50 to 60, these trees are fully grown but still have another century of life if they escape wildfires, windstorms, and insect-borne diseases.

While lodgepoles can be part of larger communities of trees, they grow more often in thick stands on their own, especially here. Attributes that are often liabilities (relatively thin bark, shallow roots) are assets for lodgepoles in compromised habitat. Thicker-barked, deeper-rooted trees cannot tolerate common Yellowstone conditions: acidic, rhyolitic soils and incursion of thermal groundwater.

They're also monoecious, having both male and female cones on the same tree. Catkins (male

Above, from left: Lodgepole pine bark is thin and flaky and tends to be highly variegated in terms of color, ranging from an orangey-brown to gray and black.

Lodgepole pine needles, cones, and catkins.

cones) don't look like cones at all, but long, thin, soft half-inch strands clustered on branches in spring when they produce pollen. Female cones look like what you'd expect, growing in whorls of two to five and to lengths of half an inch. As with other pines, these contain ovules which become seeds when fertilized by pollen, each producing 40 to 50. Individual trees reach sexual maturity between 5 and 10 years old. Young lodgepoles may bear few cones, if any, while mature specimens can drop upwards of 500.

Also notable of Rocky Mountain lodgepoles is cone polymorphism: the same tree can produce two different types of female cones, which helps boost reproductive diversity. Open (non-serotinous) cones are more common; they drop seeds annually, maintaining lodgepole's dominance in Yellowstone. Closed (serotinous) cones, on the other hand, remain sealed by their own resin and can only drop seeds when melted open by extreme heat from periodic forest fires. These closed cones may remain sealed tight for years or decades on the forest floor, but their seeds are still viable and germinate easily on newly cleared ground after a fire. Lodgepole stands where non-serotinous cones predominate tend to contain mixed ages of trees, while forests with high levels of serotiny tend toward more even-aged stands that develop together from the flush of seedlings that follow a fire.

Historically, so-called stand replacement fires have swept through parts of Yellowstone every 150 to 400 years, but as the climate heats up, these blazes are becoming more frequent—every 25 to 60 years. Lodgepole forests allowed sufficient time to recuperate from major burns on the old timeframe— over a century or more—are more likely to thrive than those that burn on these shorter intervals. A 2019 study found with more frequent fires, seedling density fell sixfold, and wood biomass dropped upwards of 60 percent, compared with the longer intervals of the past. Researchers worry these indicators may signal less resilient forests and a long-term trend toward less tree cover and reduced biodiversity across Greater Yellowstone ecosystems; only time will tell.

The forest parts, the river comes into view, and sagebrush crowds the understory. Ignore a turnoff to the right (you'll visit that section later) and head toward the river, which you'll reach shortly. Rocks called glacial erratics are scattered about the riverbed, in grassy midstream islets and along the banks on both sides of the Madison; you'll dodge a few as you hike. In late spring and early summer, silky lupines spice up the color palette here with signature purple sprigs. Meanwhile, clusters of spreading phlox resemble fireworks displays of white stars. Threadleaf sedge, smooth brome, and kinnikinnick fill out this diverse, mature riparian understory.

The source of the Madison lies about 10 miles to the east, at the confluence of the Gibbon and Firehole rivers—the so-called Madison Junction. Given those source rivers are partially fed by heated thermal features, the Madison runs much warmer than the average river at such a high elevation, with summertime water temps often topping 70°.

Cold temps of most alpine rivers also mean they're somewhat devoid of organic nutrients, but the Madison teems with wildlife. It's warm enough for plants that attract fish, not to mention fishermen, and nature lovers of all stripes.

Below, from left: On a clear day, a hike on the Two Ribbons Trail yields views across the Madison River to the stately Gallatin Range (elevation roughly 10,000 feet), ten miles to the north.

Kinnikinnick, a native shrub, is one of the hardy understory plants you'll see along forested sections of Two Ribbons Trail.

Continue along the river, admiring its rushing waters and the panorama beyond: sagebrush meadow backed by the stately Gallatin Range about 10 miles north. If you're tired, or even if you're not, avail yourself of one of the benches the park service has installed here to encourage you to take a moment to contemplate. You're much more likely to spot wildlife—perhaps an osprey or bald eagle fishing—if you're stationary.

If it's a warm summer day and you're tempted to take a dip in the shallow current, go for it. (Keep an eye on kids and pets who could get washed away.)

When you've dried off, continue along the boardwalk until it forks right, back into the forest, to pick up the other ribbon in question and loop back to base. You'll soon enter a deeper, darker forest, where many small lodgepoles (less than 12 feet) jockey for every inch of available real estate.

The reason is this strip of land was decimated during wildfires in 1988. That horrific summer saw eight massive fires scorch almost 800,000 acres, or 36 percent of the total land base, of Yellowstone National Park. Federal, state, and local authorities deployed some 25,000 firefighters to battle the blazes and protect important natural features, as well as structures and facilities, at a cost of $120 million—a valiant response to an epic natural nightmare.

While the major fires of 1988 started in the northeast corner of the park during a particularly dry June, flames didn't reach this stretch until early September, when the North Fork Fire expanded rapidly. The last (and eventually largest) of the eight blazes, the North Fork Fire ignited in late July when a woodcutter discarded a lit cigarette in Caribou-Targhee National Forest, just outside the park's western border.

Decades of supposed fire suppression had actually led to a preponderance of tinder on the forest floor. This combined with drought and heavy winds meant the blaze quickly spread to 400,000-plus acres, threatening buildings and facilities near Madison, Norris, and Canyon junctions before shifting west, where it burned through sections of the Madison River Valley toward the park's western entrance—including this stretch now known as the Two Ribbons Trail. While dozens of structures were saved, human intervention did nothing to stop the spread overall, and the North Fork Fire burned until snow and rain put out the flames for good the second week of September.

While you can still see the effects of the blaze around the park, few are as telling as this ribbon of lodgepole forest between the Madison River and US Highway 191. As you walk this half-mile stretch, the contrast between larger,

◂ Silky lupine produces showy purple floral spikes in late spring and early summer.

A lodgepole pine sapling represents a new generation of forest growing up in land cleared by the 1988 fires. ▸

unburned mature trees, the jumble of saplings, and blackened standing and fallen pines is striking. If it weren't for the boardwalk, you couldn't hope to traverse such a dense thicket.

The short, stout trees in this dense stand are mostly three decades old, springing from seeds inside serotinous cones released by the heat of the North Fork Fire in 1988. Fireweed, silky lupine, common juniper, and thinleaf huckleberry work their way into the understory here, the dense stands of lodgepoles crowding out most others.

After a quarter-mile, you'll rejoin the main trail. Turn left, and shortly you're back at the trailhead. If the Two Ribbons Trail was your first exposure to the wonders of Yellowstone, you've got so much more to see and learn about the world's first national park! And if you've been here before, perhaps you'll see the park with fresh eyes, having learned firsthand about forces of nature.

MADISON JUNCTION
AND
YELLOWSTONE'S CREATION MYTH

A dozen miles east of Two Ribbons Trail, the Gibbon and Firehole rivers join to form the Madison River. This junction is now a sacred spot in the history of both the United States and the national park ideal, given what transpired there on September 19, 1870. A group of explorers (known as the Washburn Expedition) representing various railroad and government interests gathered around their campfire at Madison Junction that night and supposedly first broached the idea of preserving Yellowstone as the world's first national park.

But historians have cast doubt on whether the genesis of the national parks idea (or ideal) really sprung from this campfire discussion. In their 2003 book *Myth and History in the Creation of Yellowstone National Park*, Paul Schullery and Lee Whittlesey make a compelling case that the idea of preserving Yellowstone and future areas of outstanding natural character as preserves emerged long before that early fall night in 1870.

Regardless of the veracity of Yellowstone's creation myth, the fact that members of the influential Washburn Expedition recommended setting aside an area so rich in resources and potential private wealth was indeed a societal milestone; it no doubt contributed to Congress' willingness to officially designate Yellowstone the world's first national park a year and half later. Madison Junction will surely remain one of the most sacred spots in the world for those who love and want to protect nature and the outdoors.

FIREHOLE CANYON ROAD

Short side trip off the Grand Loop to a waterfall and canyon between ancient lava flows

DIFFICULTY
Easy

DRIVE LENGTH
2 miles

LOCATION
West-Central Yellowstone (Madison)

D rive this one-way paved road—part of the old stage-coach route through Yellowstone that preceded the Grand Loop Road—for two quick miles as it cuts through a verdant lodgepole forest, skirts a monumental canyon and waterfall, and drops you at a rare sanctioned Yellowstone swimming hole before spilling back out onto the Grand Loop Road.

You can pick up one-lane, one-way Firehole Canyon Road a half mile south of Madison Junction. RVs and tour buses aren't allowed on this narrow, twisty single-lane road, so you'll lose at least some of the crowd. After about a third of a mile, the road turns from west to south, hugging the eastern banks of the Firehole River.

There isn't much space between your car and the river for much of this ride. Some stretches have a single row of lodgepole pines—a few others have rough-hewn cattle fencing around particularly dangerous curves. But other stretches offer no such guardrails, so go slow and drive carefully.

After another two-thirds of a mile, pull into the small parking area on the left (east) side of the road, and carefully cross on foot to the other side. Below is Firehole Falls, stair-stepping 40 feet through Firehole Canyon in all its geologic glory. You're standing in a spot where a flow

of molten rhyolite lava, the 114,000-year-old West Yellowstone Flow, met and cooled against the older, already solidified Nez Perce Creek Flow (160,000 years old). The fast-moving Firehole River travels the chasm in between.

Unlike the dramatic volcanic eruption that created the Yellowstone Caldera hundreds of millennia earlier, these rhyolite (or granite-forming) walls of lava here at Firehole Canyon oozed slowly over the surface, moving at most a few hundred feet per day, for months or even years on end—and destroying everything in their paths. The rock that makes up the West Yellowstone Flow on the opposite side rises 800 feet above Firehole Canyon. It's as much as 1150 feet thick in other spots along its 1-mile footprint.

While the trip these rock faces made to get here may not have been long, it was arduous. Look at the rocks up close and you'll notice they're riddled with pockmarks, essentially the skeletal remains of gas bubbles effervescing through the lava before it cooled and settled. Different swaths of rock face take on different shades of brown, beige, and blue-gray

▴ Firehole Falls tumbles 40 feet in the middle of Firehole Canyon.

Above, from left: Elegant sunburst lichen and common juniper lend some color to the gray granite rock face.

Firehole Canyon came to be 114,000 years ago when the West Yellowstone Flow of rhyolite lava cooled along the banks of the Firehole River.

depending on where surface and groundwater vaporized as it encountered the still hot, slow-moving flow.

Some of these faces are covered in elegant sunburst lichen, an orange-red spreader well-suited to colonizing rock substrates at these elevations. (Firehole Falls sits at 6900 feet above sea level.) Not all lichens degrade their substrate, but elegant sunburst does. In the process of making a living, this lichen releases small amounts of acid into the host rock that lead to chemical weathering, which causes the granite to slowly disintegrate.

Seeing such lava flows up close makes it easier to understand how the unique landscapes and landforms of Yellowstone came to be. Indeed, more than 30 different rhyolitic lava flows—like the two here—have essentially filled the massive 1350-square-mile hole created by the Yellowstone supervolcano 630,000 years ago. And the fact Yellowstone is still so geothermally active means the landscapes are still in a state of flux. The specter of another cataclysmic eruption here looms large, but geologists aren't convinced there's enough molten magma left belowground for another such event. Elsewhere, volcanic systems do not produce more than one super-eruption in their lifetimes, so chances are slim that it could happen again here.

That said, Yellowstone isn't like other places. The big blast 630,000 years ago was actually the *third* super-eruption in the immediate vicinity of Yellowstone; the previous two were similarly destructive or reformative. Each preceded the subsequent super-eruption by about 700,000 years. While volcanoes don't erupt on schedules, we *are* coming up soon on another interval of approximately 700,000 years . . .

But don't let this stop you from visiting Yellowstone now. Advances in the geological sciences and volcanology have allowed us to keep an eye on seismic activity in the area, which should afford humans in or around Yellowstone plenty of advance warning and time to evacuate. Only geologic time will tell if another super-eruption is in store here, let alone whether the Yellowstone of the future looks anything like the Yellowstone of today. The one thing we can be sure of is volcanoes are unpredictable.

When you've had enough canyon and waterfall viewing, continue driving south on Firehole Canyon Road. In about a mile, the river and road curve east, and you'll see a wide shoulder and a couple of changing booths to the left (north). If it's a warm summer day and the trail down to the Firehole River swimming area is open, park the car on the widened shoulder if you can find a spot, and follow the wooden stairway across the road down to the rocky riverside beach below.

▲ A thick forest of lodgepole pines now covers the West Yellowstone Flow.

Swimming is generally frowned upon in Yellowstone given its profusion of acidic, heated thermal springs, so the fact the National Park Service allows it in this calm stretch of the Firehole is a welcome treat. While the riparian environment makes for an appealing setting for a chilly swim, crowds on warm summer days can detract from the experience. Whether or not you want to get wet, it's at least worth a stop.

Back in the car, follow the road another quarter mile and fork to the right to check out the Cascades of the Firehole, where the river pours out over a granite ledge rife with odd-sized boulders, fallen trees, and other wild obstructions. If you didn't feel off the beaten path before, now you really will. If immersion in nature escaped you at the crowded swimming area, you may find it here (minus swimming) in this slightly wilder corner.

The Cascades of the Firehole is a warmup for the 40-foot drop up ahead at Firehole Falls. ▸

In late spring and early summer, you'll notice silky lupine, which sends up purple-blue shoots to attract bees, its only pollinator. These plants also fix nitrogen in the soil, which acts as a natural fertilizer for other flora. Another plant found in relative abundance here is common juniper. This low-slung shrub in the cypress family typically only grows to about four feet but spreads horizontally a good 10 feet in many cases here. Its berries in late summer and fall are beloved by both black and grizzly bears; birds, including pine grosbeaks, mountain chickadees, American robins, and Bohemian waxwings; and of course, humans enamored of martinis. (Juniper berries are a primary ingredient in the process of distilling gin).

Enjoy the serenity and sounds of rushing water through the trees at this last stop in the canyon. When you're ready to rejoin the beaten path, drive back out of the Cascades dead-end and take a quick right onto Firehole Canyon Road, which terminates in a few more feet at the junction with the Grand Loop Road.

The whole drive delivers plenty of scenic bang for the buck in its short, two-mile course, not to mention important lessons on volcanism in the world's first national park. Swimming is a bonus for those who can brave the crowds and icy waters. Given that drive time is only about 10 minutes, there may not be a quicker way off the beaten path in all of Yellowstone National Park.

MONUMENT GEYSER BASIN

Short but steep forest hike to a wild, off-the-beaten-path, mountain-clad geyser basin

DIFFICULTY
Easy to Moderate

LOCATION
West-Central Yellowstone
(between Madison and Norris)

HIKE LENGTH
2.5 miles

I f you like beautiful hikes and thermal features but hate crowds, Monument Geyser Basin could be your favorite destination in Yellowstone. The mile-long hike up into this remote subalpine basin ensures you won't cross paths with anyone from the sandals-and-boardwalk set. Your reward for hoofing it all the way up there—three quarters of a mile gains 650 feet in elevation!—is that you might just have this otherworldly spot all to yourself.

The trail to Monument Geyser Basin couldn't start out any more sublime, following the west bank of the red rhyolite-lined Gibbon River as it twists and turns for a half mile among young lodgepole pines growing mostly from ashes of the 1988 fires. Some sections of the trail bisect burn zones marked by standing dead lodgepole trunks, chalky gray and black yet showing no signs of giving up their spots anytime soon.

Heartleaf arnica, an herbaceous groundcover recognizable for its heart-shaped leaves, lines the trail and

The shallow, fast-moving Gibbon River is a great place to fly fish or just watch trout swim on by. ▾

Clockwise from top: Western serviceberry dresses up the mid-canopy, especially its showy white flowers in late spring and early summer.

Variegated yellow pond-lily adorns a quiet stretch of Gibbon River shoreline.

Western bracken fern dresses up the forest floor.

spreads between trunks. If you're here in early to midsummer, prepare to be dazzled by the plant's bright yellow, sunflowery blooms, each sporting seven to twelve triple-pointed petals surrounding a honeycomb-like central rosette. Western bracken fern and cow parsnip peek up above other groundcovers to gather a little light in the rocky, rough and tumble soil. Western serviceberry reaches the understory, its showy white flowers accompanied by many others in early summer.

As the trail flirts with the river, look for variegated yellow pond-lily, with its green oval-shaped leathery pads and erect bulbous yellow flowers. American beavers, mallards, and mule deer are among the wildlife that love to munch on these aquatic plants.

This section of the river is a popular fly-fishing spot, as the undercut banks and riffling waters are chock full of trout. If you have a valid National Park Service fishing permit and it's between June and October, you can take as many rainbows, browns, or brookies as you want—all non-native, introduced species plentiful in the river

system. But native cutthroats, which the park service is working to restore around Yellowstone, are strictly catch and release. (If a fish has two red slash marks under its gills, it's a cutthroat. Let it live.)

⌃ Anglers can keep any non-native trout they catch in the Gibbon River, which was stocked for fishing more than a century ago.

CUTTHROAT REDUX

A dozen species of fish once populated the Yellowstone watershed, each evolved for unique conditions and environments through speciation—when one group diverges from others of its species and evolves traits to match its environment. These include Arctic grayling, mountain whitefish, and cutthroat trout.

In order to enhance recreational opportunities and encourage visitation, early park managers stocked Yellowstone's waterways with non-native trout. Given the inevitable intermingling between subspecies where their habitats overlapped, these interlopers—brown, brook, rainbow, and lake trout—preyed on native cutthroats, outcompeted them for limited aquatic resources, and also hybridized with them, essentially reducing the genetic diversity and evolutionary resilience of the larger watershed.

By the 1930s, park managers realized the damage caused by non-native fish stocking here and curtailed the practice. But overzealous and indiscriminate stocking of native Yellowstone cutthroats

▲ Park managers are working to restore populations of Westslope cutthroat trout, a native fish abundant in Yellowstone from the end of the last ice age until around 1900. Thanks to a variety of factors, today the fish occupies only 5 percent of its former range.

both within and beyond their original range into the 1950s still plagues marine ecosystems throughout the park. This influx of one species has made it difficult for other native species to hang on, given the increased competition for resources and inevitability of interbreeding.

Various management techniques—especially an evolving set of restrictions on fish harvesting—have helped fish like Westslope cutthroats and Arctic grayling stage comebacks in some of their ancestral home waters. While no one alive today will likely ever see a Yellowstone National Park devoid of non-native fish, we've learned a lot. Hopefully native cutthroats will be abundant by the time our grandkids are fishing the Gibbon. Until then, if you catch one with red slashes under its gills, throw it back to live another day.

If you see a small songbird flitting about along the waterline, it may well be an American dipper, North America's only true aquatic songbird. They nest on cliffs near rivers and streams. The brown-tinged heads on these stocky gray birds are highlighted with white eyelid feathers, so their eyes flash white when they blink. Preening releases natural

◂ Young lodgepole pines have sprung up amidst the wholesale destruction wrought by the 1988 fires.

oil that helps keep their feathers waterproof, enabling them to dive into cold water in search of aquatic insects. They fish like this throughout winter thanks to their low metabolic rate, extra oxygen-carrying capacity in their blood, and a surprisingly thick coat of feathers. Indeed, dippers catch all of their food underwater in swift streams by swimming and walking on the bottom.

At about the half-mile point, the trail hairpins to the left and begins climbing away from the river and nearby road into dense, fire-scarred forest. As the trail gains elevation, evidence of the 1988 fires is everywhere, with a mix of live and dead lodgepoles, and the forest floor a jumbled mess of downed timber and dogged groundcover flora.

From the kink in the trail to Monument Geyser Basin, you'll gain 650 feet in elevation over less than three-quarters of a mile. You'll feel it going up. If it's a warm day, bring plenty of water and take as many rest stops as you need.

You'll know you're close by the now familiar scent of sulfur. Before you know it, the trail opens into an expanse populated by steaming vents, erupting geysers, and thin-crusted thermally heated ground: welcome to Monument Geyser Basin. The otherworldly landscape is dusted in white by the constant outpouring of mineral-laden water and steam emanating from 30-plus thermal features—including vents, fumaroles, mudpots, and geyser cones—over the 4-plus-acre basin between forested hillsides. Leftover minerals form thin, brittle sinter deposits, making cross-basin foot travel treacherous. Most of the geyser cones here are dormant, but a few actively belch out steam and water constantly or at intervals. Let the sounds of hissing and underground bubbling be a warning not to stray far from solid ground.

Look south across the white crusty expanse and you'll see Monument Geyser, the namesake thermal feature of this basin, its white cone rising about 8 feet above the fray and puffing pasty steam sporadically throughout the day. Every now and then it erupts, ejecting super-hot water 1 to 2 feet into the air. While it's no Old Faithful, Monument's belch is a cool sight up here in this subalpine moonscape.

One of the joys of visiting this geyser basin is that you are free to wander without boardwalks, fences, or signs. This

Below, from left:
A lichen-encrusted glacial erratic boulder.

Creeping barberry is beloved by pollinators for its yellow spring blooms and by birds for the berries that follow.

Watch where you step once you reach Monument Geyser Basin; there are no boardwalks to guide you or fences to keep you from falling into superheated vents.

thermal wonderland is truly free range, but that means it is up to you to stay safe. Avoid stepping on any thin-crusted chalky ground that could subject your lower extremities to burns if you crack through. Steer clear of steaming streams of water that trail down into the forest. And keep clear of geyser cones, dormant or otherwise, as they could be fragile and dangerous. Also, any steam or water spewing out of Monument Geyser or any other cone could burn, so use good judgment and keep your distance.

When you've had your fill of Monument Geyser Basin, head back down the way you came. It will be much easier going down, but make sure to drink in the views that reveal Gibbon Meadows bisected by the meandering Gibbon River

▲ Geyser cones are the most visibly active thermal features at Monument Geyser Basin, spewing steam and occasionally erupting with small outbursts of superheated water.

Top Standing dead trees, casualties of the 1988 fires, buffer each side of the trail to Monument Geyser Basin.

Above Lodgepole pine needles growing at the edge of Monument Geyser Basin can desiccate from constant exposure to hot gases.

to the north, with Norris Geyser Basin (4 miles away as the eagle flies) further in the distance. The big peak to the northwest, 10-plus miles away, is glacier-clad Mt. Holmes (elevation 10,335 feet) in the Gallatin Range.

While Monument Geyser Basin may not have the drama of other thermal features around Yellowstone, the forested hike to get there and its wilderness feel, without the throngs of tourists, give it a special appeal all its own.

ARTISTS' PAINTPOTS

Burned-over lodgepole forest trail to multicolored thermal features reminiscent of an artist's palette

DIFFICULTY
Easy

LOCATION
Central Yellowstone (Norris)

HIKE LENGTH
1.1 miles

The 1.1-mile lollipop loop trail through the Artists' Paintpots section of Gibbon Geyser Basin is a great introduction to the different types of thermal features that contribute to Yellowstone's fame as a natural attraction. Slightly less famous than many similar features in central Yellowstone, Artists' Paintpots is accessible via a hiker-friendly trail that gets up close and personal with burned forests, steaming fumaroles, superheated springs, multi-hued pools, erupting geysers, and bubbling mudpots.

Look for the side road to Artists' Paintpots on the east side of the Grand Loop Highway, 3.5 miles south of the Norris Geyser Basin turnout. The parking lot can accommodate around 40 cars, plus another ten RVs or buses.

Start at the trailhead and hike for a third of a mile through lodgepole forest, then through a mixed area burned severely during the 1988 fires. Note one cluster of standing dead trees with white coloration around their bases, killed not by fire, but by inundation with thermal run-off during a flooding event decades ago. The floodwaters' mineral content killed these so-called "bobby socks" trees, and they've stood dead in place ever since. Plantain goldenweed, an aster cousin, boasts pretty yellow blooms in late spring and early summer and grows in small clusters at the forest edge.

Clockwise from above: Iron oxides precipitate from this reddened thermal pool at the base of Paintpot Hill.

Make your way through burned-over forest on the way to Paintpot Hill.

Paintpot Hill rises up above the iron oxide-tinged Geyser Creek.

As the trail leaves the forest, the landscape opens up, and Paintpot Hill rises ahead. This hill formed when an ancient lava flow oozed up but then did not flow, forming a rhyolite dome. Hydrothermal activity isn't done shaping this particular spot, as evidenced by its profusion of active geysers, vents, mudpots, and fumaroles.

Hop on the boardwalk loop to tour the colorful, textural thermal features that inspired the site's name. As at other thermal features in Yellowstone, stay on the boardwalk, as straying can lead to burns or worse, not to mention hefty fines, a ban from the park, and potentially jail time. A sign at the trailhead warns that twenty people have been scalded to death by stepping into the thermal features here, with hundreds more badly burned and scarred.

Follow the lollipop section of the loop in either direction—both ways lead uphill and back down. To the right, you'll pass calm, chalky blue pools fringed by sinter deposits tinted red from iron oxide precipitation. These pools' unique color comes from their depth and lack of organic

‹ An overlook at the high point on the boardwalk trail gets visitors up close and personal with boiling mudpots tucked into Paintpot Hill.

‹ The boardwalk passes some chalky blue "paint pots" fringed with red on the way to Paintpot Hill. Mt. Holmes rises above the Yellowstone caldera some five miles to the northeast.

inhabitants, as their temps are inhospitable to most plants, animals, and even bacteria.

A bit further on, you'll pass a series of large, brown creamy mudpots fueled by steaming, gurgling vents. Mudpots form as hydrogen sulfide gas emanating from underground sources is converted by microorganisms into sulfuric acid, which in turn breaks down the rhyolitic rock into clay. As more gas bubbles up from below, the mud appears to boil.

These mudpots' location tucked into the hillside keeps them sludgier than features down below, where water pools. And iron oxides and other minerals lend them a pink tinge, depending on the time of year and other conditions. Stay on the boardwalk and overlook platforms, and keep an eye out for flying mud—although not actually boiling, it could still burn exposed skin.

The consistency of these mudpots also changes with the seasons. Soupy in spring, thickening to a stew in summer—sometimes, by late summer, especially in a very dry year, they dry up and become parched patches punctuated by steam vents (fumaroles) instead of the gurglers you'd expect to see there.

Revel in gurgling mudpots at your leisure, then head down the other way. Descending, you'll notice you've gained

• Blood Geyser paints the landscape as it sends streams of iron oxide-tinged water down Paintpot Hill.

• Plantain gold-enweed thrives where most other herbaceous plants couldn't survive—in thermally compromised acidic soils like those around Artists' Paintpots and other thermal features in Yellowstone.

enough elevation to gather a view of the thermal features downhill and beyond, across the Gibbon River Valley to Gibbon Meadows, another thermally active area (and a favorite hangout for Rocky Mountain elk). You'll pass several more small pools and vents on your way.

But perhaps the most striking feature of the hike comes next: Blood Geyser, a 10-by-13-foot pool named for the red-tinged mineral deposits around its perimeter. This feature has bubbled and steamed constantly since at least 1882, occasionally erupting to around six feet and discharging some 150 gallons of water per minute. Its underground feeder spring keeps the pool full, even as excess water runs off in a scalding stream, merging into Geyser Creek and eventually the Gibbon River. This and other thermal sources endow the nearby stretch of the Gibbon with a special appeal for anglers looking to score brownies (non-native brown trout), which thrive in the more temperate waters.

Pass some more steaming pools, and soon enough you'll be back where the boardwalk began. Retrace your steps to the parking lot.

You won't be sorry you checked out Artists' Paintpots—this trail packs a lot of thermal action into a small package without the crowds of nearby geyser basins. Indeed, it might be one of the best places to drink in the sights, sounds, and smells of America's original wonderland.

NORRIS GEYSER BASIN

Steaming vents, geysers, and rainbows highlight the hottest and most dynamic of Yellowstone's thermal spots

DIFFICULTY
Easy

LOCATION
Central Yellowstone (Norris)

HIKE LENGTH
1.5 miles

Norris Geyser Basin in central Yellowstone is a place of extremes in a land of extremes, and walking its steaming, bubbling, gushering, and sometimes-technicolor expanse is an experience unlike any other on the planet. Plus, if you happen to be there at the right time, you could witness the world's tallest active geyser erupt.

This well-marked site is located at the junction of Highway 89 and Norris Canyon Road. The parking lot can fit about 100 cars, with another section that accommodates a dozen or so buses or RVs. While this sounds like plenty, it fills up during summer high season—go early if you can—but don't let that scare you. Norris Geyser Basin is just big enough to accommodate a full parking lot of people and still offer a little breathing room on its extensive boardwalk network. While this hydrothermal hotspot is hardly off the beaten path, it's not nearly as crowded as some.

Follow the sandy trail on the lot's west side through a copse of lodgepole pines, where you'll pass a little park bookstore booth and a small, rustic museum structure with interpretive exhibits about Norris Geyser Basin. Once you've browsed and checked the trail map there to get your bearings, head toward the boardwalk to the south to tackle the larger, more dynamic Back Basin, a 1.5-mile loop. On your way, note a few dead lodgepole pines that look like they're wearing bobby socks. These snags soak up mineral-laden hydrothermal water that eventually evaporates, leaving the minerals behind to color the base of the trees' trunks white.

In a few steps, the steaming moonscape of Back Basin spreads out before you. Trail soon meets boardwalk and brings you into intimate terms with the Hades-like surroundings. You'll notice right off that trees are scarce in the thermal areas here compared to Upper Geyser Basin, Biscuit Basin, and others. The water underground here is so hot that surrounding soils are inhospitable to even hardy, rhyolitic-soil-loving trees like lodgepoles.

◂ The trail cuts through some lodgepole pines on its way to Norris Geyser Basin.

Soon you'll arrive at Emerald Spring, a steaming yet placid blue-green splotch on your right. This 27-foot-deep pool gets its dazzling shade from a combination of the water absorbing all the colors of sunlight except blue (which is reflected back to your eyes) and crystallized yellow sulfur deposits from mineral precipitation lining its interior. The resulting emerald color of the water is what you get when these two hues combine, sort of like how a painter can mix blue and yellow to get green.

Continuing south on the boardwalk, in .2 miles, follow the side trail to your left to a viewing platform overlooking Steamboat Geyser, the tallest active geyser in the world. This monstrous spouter shoots a superheated band of water as high as 380 feet, but not according to any discernible schedule. In 2018, Steamboat roared back to life after four years of dormancy, working its way up to 48 eruptions a year in both 2019 and 2020. These days the geyser (whose exhalations reminded early explorers of a steamship's) has settled a little but is still in an eruptive phase, blowing around 20 times a year at random intervals.

When Steamboat goes, it goes big, usually beginning with a rumble people hear for miles around. Next, water surges from the geyser's two vents. When enough pressure builds, it first sends torrents of water skyward, followed by seemingly endless amounts of steam. The gushing water deposits a fine layer of silica on everything in its path, sometimes including cars in the parking area about 700 feet north. (At least if your car gets doused, presumably you got to see the world's tallest geyser erupt—and insurance will probably cover the damage.)

There's little sense in planning around a potential eruption at Steamboat, but since you're already here, you may as well stand by for a few minutes, just in case. When you've given up, return to the boardwalk and you'll soon pass Cistern Spring, a dazzlingly blue, constantly overflowing pool. The only time the water in Cistern doesn't overflow its sinter banks is when Steamboat erupts. The two are hydrothermally linked, and the big geyser drains the water from surrounding underground channels.

Continue past a number of other noteworthy thermal features whose names say it all: Black Pit Spring, Crater Spring, Root Pool, Tantalus Geyser, Dishwater Spring,

Mud Spring, Black Hermit Caldron, Green Dragon Spring, and Blue Mud Steam Vent.

The next Back Basin feature is second only to Steamboat Geyser in terms of notoriety. Porkchop Geyser, about halfway down the loop, is named for its shape. It rose to prominence in 1989, when after years of perpetual eruptions from a mostly dry crater, it exploded with great force to a height that topped 100 feet. This blast threw boulders bigger than beach balls more than 200 feet away and created a new crater in the process. Luckily no one was hurt, but it serves as a reminder of how unpredictable and hazardous hydrothermal features can be.

After the commotion, Porkchop Geyser went back to sleep, not to be heard from again until 2003. On July 11 that year, park staff noticed dramatic increases in hydrothermal activity around the Back Basin: rising water temperatures; water in longstanding thermal pools suddenly boiling away, leaving only hissing steam vents; the formation of new mud pots; and the sudden death of trees and other vegetation. During this buildup, water temperatures in Porkchop's vents rose from their typical 152°F to 190°F. On July 16, Porkchop erupted again for the first time in 15 years.

Cut to the 2020s, and Porkchop Geyser has settled as a gently roiling hot spring. Only time will tell if and when things heat up again—it could be tomorrow; it could be in 100 years.

Thanks to its extreme heat and potentially hazardous dynamism, no other geyser basin in the world is monitored as closely or studied as much as Norris. Learning what makes these more extreme hydrothermal features tick helps scientists learn more about volcanism generally, specifically

These National Park Service photos show Porkchop Geyser in September 1984 (left) and August 1986 (right); the geyser entered a period of near-constant eruption in the interim, and its pool disappeared before it exploded on September 5, 1989. ▾

1984　　1986

Norris Geyser Basin may not be hell, but it sure looks that way.

how to recognize when changes at a given hydrothermal area are cause for concern (and evacuation).

Furthermore, this research has yielded knowledge about the very essence of life and gives us hope that life could exist on other planets. While the majority of thermophiles—organisms that thrive in extreme environments—discovered around Norris Geyser Basin derive their energy from photosynthesis like other plants, a select few survive instead on a steady diet of dissolved metals and hydrogen found in the highly acidic pore water of the rock underlying the basin. Indeed, a 2005 study by researchers from the University of Colorado, Boulder found that microbes living here in hot springs with water temperatures averaging greater than 158° rely on hydrogen as their primary fuel source. Some of these may have been the first types of life forms on this planet during Earth's explosive early days. Scientists take note of the fossil imprints made here by these relatively unique microbes so they can look for similar evidence in the remnants of ancient geothermal environments on Mars or elsewhere.

Continuing through the Back Basin, pass Rubble Geyser, then Palpitator Spring, Fearless Geyser, Monarch Geyser, and Branch Spring. Next up is Minute Geyser, which used to erupt like clockwork every 60 seconds, but since its western vent was clogged with rocks thrown in by irresponsible visitors decades ago—the park's main road used to pass within 70 feet of the trail here—it only goes off every now and again from its smaller eastern vent.

Next up, check out Forgotten Fumarole and Rediscovered Geyser before the boardwalk curves to the east and returns to the beginning of the Back Basin loop. If you've had enough of Norris Geyser Basin, you can head back to the parking lot from here. If you're craving more hydrothermal action, don't miss Norris' other boardwalk network, a .75-mile loop around Porcelain Basin.

Head north and go left (west) at the first junction of Porcelain Basin. Immediately you'll notice most of the ground ahead of you is covered by veil-like sheets of milky mineral deposits called siliceous sinter (also known as geyserite), which precipitates to the surface via the bubbling, boiling water that underlies the basin. The profusion and constant replenishment of sinter here plays an active role in keeping Norris Geyser Basin one of the most dynamic areas in the region by sealing off some hot springs and geysers, forcing hot pressurized water underground to find weak spots elsewhere to blow through.

Look north to see a clustered assortment of geothermal features—Valentine Geyser, Dark Cavern Geyser, Guardian Geyser Steam Vent, Black Growler Steam Vent, Ledge Geyser, and Jetsam Pool—none more than 200 feet away from the boardwalk. From where you stand, you may as well be in hell. But hold on, you've been good . . . It's just another walk in Yellowstone National Park.

Continue through this geothermal spectacle, and keep an eye out for Glacial Melt Geyser at right and then Crackling Lake just to the left. The latter is named for popping sounds that emanate from springs on its far shore. Keep moving north past Whale's Mouth, which resembles a whale's gullet; the boardwalk then curves and dead-ends at an overlook of Pinwheel Geyser.

From here, the boardwalk turns south, and soon you'll see Whirligig Geyser, nowadays more of an inactive spring than a spouter, covered in various thermophilic algae and cyanobacteria arrayed in bright green to orange red to white-streaked. These simplistic, unicellular prehistoric life forms only exist in highly sulfuric hot springs like these,

Opposite, clockwise from top: Norris Geyser Basin is one of the most colorful spots in Yellowstone thanks to its extreme geothermal features.

Horse dung fungus may not look pretty, but it provides valuable environmental services, including carbon dioxide sequestration.

The Whale's Mouth is a striking shade of milky blue-green.

and their color display is second to none, so get a good look while you can.

Fungi are another life form that play important roles in thermal ecology. Look out for horse dung fungus, which fruits in the likeness of its namesake and produces nitrogen, benefitting surrounding plants, and gets back carbon in return.

Next up is Fireball Geyser, and behind it, Pinto Geyser. A few feet later, look for Scummy Pool on the right and

⊳ Lodgepole pines, not welcome in the boiling expanse, crowd the sidelines of Norris Geyser Basin.

Sunday Geyser and Colloidal Pool to the left. If you spot some pink-orange mounds on top of the thermophilic mats here, you are looking at the nests of ephydrid flies. These little black flies top out at a quarter inch and sustain themselves by eating the very algae that provides their habitat. Rather than depleting the algae below them, ephydrid flies' consumption actually stimulates more matting. While the flies create habitat for themselves in this way, they also open themselves up to increased predation by spiders and beetles by providing easy access across the top of otherwise scalding hot springs.

Hook a left at the next fork and see Hurricane Vent before continuing on for far-off views of Blue Geyser. Ignore the next fork and follow the boardwalk to a dead end at an overlook of Incline Geyser and steaming, sinter-covered Porcelain Springs beyond. Backtrack to the previous fork and turn left (south), passing serene and pale blue (sometimes brown and roiling) Congress Pool on your way back to the Porcelain Basin trailhead.

If you completed both boardwalk loops at Norris Geyser Basin, you'll have hiked 2.25 miles and experienced some of the most extreme, active hydrothermal features in the national park. No doubt you'll have also learned a lot about the dynamics of Yellowstone's landscapes and gained a renewed respect for the power and unpredictability of Mother Nature.

ICE LAKE

A short hike through a lodgepole burn zone to a shallow, peaceful alpine lake

This short hike is an off-the-beaten-path treat that show-cases the destruction caused by the 1988 fires and the amazing ecosystem regeneration ever since—capped off with a stop along the shoreline of a small, shallow, forest-fringed alpine lake. It's a short, flat, family-friendly hike, but remember, you're at 8000 feet in elevation, so take it slow if it's your first or second day in the park and you're not acclimated.

Park at the small pullout with spaces for about a dozen cars on the north side of Norris-Canyon Road (3.5 miles east of Norris Geyser Basin), and begin hiking on the well-marked trail that heads north into the woods.

This dense lodgepole pine forest was hit hard during the Yellowstone fires of 1988, evidenced by the many mature lodgepoles here that are now dead. Some ashen gray "ghost trees" still stand; these tree snags are beloved as shelter by many forms of wildlife. But the majority of the ghost trees lie helter-skelter at odd angles, and this disarray of lodgepole trunks and undergrowth makes off-trail travel here ill-advised. Luckily, the Park Service keeps the main trail clear of obstructions.

Sedges like this line the shore of Ice Lake. ▾

In between all of these fallen trunks, a few surviving mature trees persist, but most of the gaps are filled by young lodgepoles. In fact, researchers found that within five years

of the 1988 fires, eight times as many lodgepole saplings established themselves in the same amount of terrain in the park's burned-over areas where only one mature tree had lived before. One of their primary study plots was in the woods right near Ice Lake.

While this profusion of new growth, sprung from recharged soils post-1988, makes the forest especially dense and less inviting than an open, park-like woodland, it serves to remind us of the resilience of nature. The fresh, green pines that fill every square inch here should fill us with optimism that if we can respect the planet and its systems—and control pollution and emissions—nature can take care of itself.

Of course, the reason the forests of Yellowstone have roared back from the dead so well is that lodgepole pines, the trees that thrive best in the park's rhyolitic soils, have evolved along with periodic wildfire. Indeed, a varying proportion of cones from any given lodgepole pine are serotinous (closed) and rely on big burns to open. Biologists think the proportion of serotinous cones may come down to the type of major disturbance that affected that parent pine's patch of forest, however many years, decades, or centuries earlier. Data shows that lodgepole stands growing from previous burns show a higher percentage of serotiny than those last disturbed by storms, earthquakes, or other non-fire insults. It's incredible the trees can take cues from the environment and alter their reproductive strategy accordingly.

Hike straight through the trees and head right at the fork in about a tenth of a mile. Soon you'll detect the glint of sunshine off water through the lodgepoles to your left, and

‹ A lodgepole sapling pops up through the chaotic jumble of the forest floor.

Below, from left: Young and younger: lodgepole pines as far as the eye can see.

Either fork in the trail leads to the shoreline of lovely little Ice Lake.

in another few steps, you'll be standing on a point ("Campsite 4D1") on the southern shoreline of Ice Lake. Campers with backcountry permits from the National Park Service can pitch a tent and spend the night here, but chances are you'll have this idyllic spot all to yourself, save for water birds and maybe an errant Shiras moose.

It's hard not to appreciate the serene beauty spread out before you from the water's edge. This shallow, 60-acre lake is only about a tenth of a mile across but stretches nearly three-quarters of a mile east to west in a roughly rectangular, kidney-bean shape. Ghost lodgepoles lance out into the water from the shoreline here and there. The sandy-bottomed lake is as clear as clear gets and looks shallow enough to wade all the way across.

In precious spots around the lake where lodgepoles haven't crowded everything else out, willows and quaking aspens jockey for position, while grouse whortleberry and various sedges fill the understory. Heartleaf arnica, with its signature heart-shaped green leaves and showy yellow summertime blooms, competes with wild strawberry and other herbaceous natives for cameo spots on the forest floor.

While there are no fish to speak of in Ice Lake given its lack of any inflow or outflow streams, there are lots of birds around. Keep an eye out for western grebes, Barrow's goldeneyes, mergansers, great blue herons, sandhill cranes, and common loons. The latter species is especially sensitive to environmental factors, and untold numbers of loons have lived shorter lives as a result of toxic metal poisoning in their home waters. The state of Wyoming considers them a "species of special concern" given their numbers have fallen some 38 percent statewide since the mid-2000s as a result of lost or contaminated habitat.

These days, 80 percent of the roughly 50 common loons left statewide call Yellowstone home. Indeed, if it weren't for the establishment and subsequent protection of Yellowstone National Park, loons would probably be long gone from this part of the Northern Rockies. Knowing this, it feels especially lucky to see or hear one in the wild. But just because loons can take refuge in Yellowstone doesn't mean they're in the clear. Wildlife managers worry that if the park's waters dry up due to ongoing drought from climate change, loons will have nowhere else to go.

If you brought a lunch or snack, this would be a good place for it. If you brought a hammock, find a couple of sturdy lodgepoles to hang it between and enjoy a little downtime. If you brought a swimsuit, the time is nigh for a dip. In mid-to-late summer, the shallow lake warms up to a tolerable temperature for swimming, and there aren't many such opportunities in Yellowstone, so get it while you can. Be aware that there are no lifeguards on duty, and more visitors to Yellowstone are injured or die from accidents in the water than from animal encounters or any other cause—don't become a statistic.

If campers or competing picnickers come along, retrace your steps back to the fork in the trail, and either head back to the car or take the other way you passed by before—it leads around to the western lakeshore for a third of a mile before intersecting with a longer backcountry trail that connects Norris Campground and Grebe Lake. If you head east at this juncture, you'll follow the north shore of Ice Lake and soon pass another sanctioned backcountry campsite (which doubles as a nice snack or lunch stop) before retracing your steps back. Regardless of how far around Ice Lake you get, you'll leave much the wiser about the ecology of wildfire, regrowth, and alpine lakes.

ROARING MOUNTAIN

Roaring Mountain in all its glory is not to be missed. This steaming mass of grayed-out earth rises about 600 feet from where you'll pull out on the east side of Grand Loop Road (Highway 89), about 5 miles north of Norris Junction. All the way up the hill's slope, volcanic vents known as fumaroles belch out puffs of steam, seemingly setting the stage for a heavy metal band. But these are nature's fog machines, and the only sound coming from this stage is the hissing of steam as it escapes the mountain's many vents.

Fumaroles are the hottest of Yellowstone's geothermal features. Any water trapped in the cracks of these vents flashes to steam immediately before it can pool on the surface, and this process causes the hissing noise that emanates from the site.

Word has it when explorers were surveying the land that was to become Yellowstone back in the 1870s, the racket coming from this hillside could be heard for miles around, thus the name "Roaring Mountain." These days, Roaring Mountain isn't nearly as loud as it used to be due to geothermal shifts underground, but if you stand nearby, you can get a feel for what the early explorers meant. Given the dynamic, unpredictable nature of Yellowstone's geothermal plumbing, Roaring Mountain may well roar again in the near future.

OBSIDIAN CLIFF

Long before Yellowstone became the world's first national park, it was known as the source of the best tool-making rock for thousands of miles around. This rare volcanic rock is called obsidian—formed around 100,000 years ago, when magma extruded from the earth's crust cooled too rapidly to trap much moisture or crystals and solidified into sharp, black glass. Obsidian was easily crafted into spear points, arrowheads, knife blades, and other tools by Indigenous peoples lucky or enterprising enough to access it.

Due to obsidian's disordered atomic structure—it has no "preferred direction of fracture"—it is easily flaked off into sharp edges, some ten times sharper than surgical steel. Yellowstone tribes made use of their obsidian reserve for practical and trade purposes and revered it as part of their spiritual practice and cultural identity.

While obsidian deposits are scattered across the American West, Yellowstone's Obsidian Cliff represents the continent's easternmost motherlode. Fragments of Yellowstone obsidian used by pre-Colombian tribes in tools have been found as far away as Washington State, the Canadian province of Alberta, Texas, and even Ohio. Indeed, the Hopewell tribe in Ohio seems to have journeyed over 1500 treacherous miles to harvest obsidian here. A walking journey like this would take years to complete.

But don't try this yourself: Obsidian Cliff is strictly off-limits to visitors, because the National Park Service knows rock hounds would make off with chunks of obsidian. There is, however, a parking area with an interpretive pullout and shelter on the opposite side of Highway 89 with a direct sightline to the monolith. The shelter was one of the first wayside exhibits in the park system. Declared a National Historic Landmark in 1996, it represents a paradigm shift in natural history education, engaging visitors directly in the field rather than through a book or museum.

From this vantage point, the big black rock rises above pretty Obsidian Creek, dominating the surrounding valley. If it's sunny, try to time your visit for mid-to-late afternoon so the 200-foot-tall rock's glassy surface and its shroud of lodgepoles are lit up by the sun's rays.

SHEEPEATER CLIFF

Columnar basalt, marmots, and
cascades among riparian willows

DIFFICULTY
Easy

LOCATION
North Yellowstone (Mammoth)

HIKE LENGTH
.75 mile

This peaceful stopover just off the Grand Loop Road about 7 miles south of Mammoth Hot Springs features scenic views of a geologically distinct rock formation and access to a beautiful riparian ecosystem, as well as the chance to see some of Yellowstone's more diminutive yet charismatic wildlife species.

From the well-marked turnoff, follow the narrow dirt access road a quarter-mile to a small parking area backing up to the cliff and picnic area. Buses, RVs, and trailers aren't allowed, giving this picnic spot a more intimate appeal than many of Yellowstone's more popular, easily accessed attractions.

‹ The colonnades of Sheepeater Cliff came into existence half a million years ago as oozing volcanic magma cooled and eroded into the hexagonal columns we see today.

As soon as you get out of the car, you'll notice crumbly but nevertheless imposing Sheepeater Cliff, standing some 50 feet high and about 150 feet wide in all its monolithic glory. Make your way past the picnic tables to the foot of the cliff, which is fronted by a jumble of big, jagged basalt chunks that have eroded off the walls and tumbled to the foreground, forming a veritable moat of rocks. Rising out of this jumble, Sheepeater Cliff may look a little like it's made of cast concrete columns—hexagonal in shape and standing side-by-side—but its form and shape couldn't be more natural.

The signature light purple color of sticky geranium's blooms livens up the palette of this otherwise brown and green landscape. ▾

Indeed, columnar basalt like this forms when volcanic magma that has oozed from the ground cools and contracts

along closely spaced fissures that work their way down into the resulting rock face, breaking it apart into the so-called colonnades we see today. Geologists trace the formation of Sheepeater Cliff to volcanic events that took place half a million years ago.

While Sheepeater Cliff has been here for eons, it got its name much more recently. Philetus Norris, second superintendent of Yellowstone National Park, passed this way in 1879 and noticed the remains of *wickiups*—traditional native dwelling structures made of tall saplings bent, driven into the ground, and tied together near the top. Norris knew this must have been a gathering spot for the Indigenous people known colloquially as Tukudeka, which translates to "sheep-eaters" in English.

This branch of the Shoshones migrated seasonally across Yellowstone's Northern Range on the hunt for Rocky Mountain bighorn sheep, as well as American bison, Rocky Mountain elk, and both mule and white-tailed deer, not to mention a wide range of edible and medicinal plants. This idyllic spot at the base of columnar basalt cliffs at the intersection of the Gardner River and Obsidian Creek was clearly one of their preferred seasonal camps. Indigenous peoples subsisted on nature's bounty here for at least 8000 years before the arrival of white people in the mid-1800s. And here in the mountainous Northern Rockies, bighorn sheep numbered in the millions—meaning there was plenty for everyone.

The Tukudeka were thought to have derived much of their dietary protein from bighorn sheep they skillfully hunted and trapped, but they also didn't let any part of the animal go to waste. They soaked rams' horns in hot water (perhaps in hot springs) to make them malleable, then straightened and joined them together with sinew in the middle to make strong bows. These big, powerful bows were prized for thousands of miles around—they could take down a bison with one skillfully administered obsidian-tipped arrow—and were often traded for more exotic goods. Sheep horns were also used to make awls, ladles, spoons, and other tools, while their hides were used for clothing, drapery, and blankets.

But white settlers flooding into the region in the late 1800s—as Indigenous peoples were moved to reservations hundreds of miles away—made a serious dent in wildlife populations with their firearms-enabled hunting techniques and hungry families to feed. By 1900, the thousands of bighorn sheep were reduced to fewer than 200 across the entirety of Yellowstone National Park.

Conservation efforts—first and foremost, the US Army banned hunting—helped bighorn numbers rebound somewhat, but to this day there are fewer than 500 individuals

Thousands of Rocky Mountain bighorn sheep used to roam Yellowstone's Northern Range; these days, only a few hundred remain. ▸

within the park, the majority in the Northern Range, which stretches from Mammoth Hot Springs east to Mt. Washburn and Specimen Ridge. These majestic ruminants fatten up on grasses, sedges, and clover in the warmer months and make do over the long, cold winter chewing on willow and sagebrush twigs.

Although overhunting decimated the region's wild bighorn population in the early days of white settlement, these days disease is a much bigger threat. Viral and bacterial infections suffered by Yellowstone's wild bighorn population typically come from domestic sheep, when the species intermingle on common grazing grounds outside park boundaries.

In the 1980s, pink eye (keratoconjunctivitis), an infectious bacteria, took a toll on bighorns throughout the park, causing temporary and sometimes permanent blindness in animals that rely on sight to navigate precipitous drop-offs and dig in the snow and dirt for precious forage. There isn't much park biologists can do about pink eye, which seems to come through in waves every few years.

Likewise, sore mouth disease (ecthyma) is a common virus in farmed sheep and goats that has also jumped into Yellowstone's bighorn population. Scabby sores around the mouth and face in ewes and lambs are a giveaway for this increasingly common ailment. The affliction doesn't usually do any permanent damage; a healthy bighorn can build up antibodies to overcome it within two to four weeks.

Nevertheless, larger outbreaks, such as in 2017, can take down weaker, smaller members of the herd who can't feed due to lesions on their mouths.

Historically, bacterial pneumonia has been an even bigger problem, first transferred from domestic sheep to their bighorn cousins when the species intermingled in foothill valleys in the late 1800s. Biologists estimate this scourge wiped out 90 percent of the bighorn population across the west by the 1920s, and numbers have never really rebounded, (despite protection from hunting, at least within park boundaries).

As commercial sheep-grazing increases in other countries and park rangers become better at keeping wild herds apart from livestock, wildlife biologists remain optimistic that disease won't sound the death knell for the species in this part of the world. While bighorns will never be as common as they were here before the arrival of white settlers, the fact that we're working to bring them back from the brink means we're on the right path now.

STALKING BIGHORN

If seeing bighorn sheep in the wild is a priority, rangers suggest starting your search in the Lamar Valley. Chances are you're saving some time to drive through the Lamar Valley anyway, given its reputation as "America's Serengeti," so why not try to add bighorn sheep to your list of wildlife to see while you're at it?

The cliffs above the confluence of the Lamar River and Soda Butte Creek are one of the park's bighorn-viewing hotspots, while another lies at the confluence of the Yellowstone and Lamar rivers (near the Yellowstone River Picnic Area). Gardner Canyon, a few miles in from the park's northern entrance, is another gathering spot for bighorns. Get out the binoculars and scan the cliff walls above you. You can also look for them on the high flanks of Mt. Washburn if you're inclined to do that epic five-mile-plus day hike.

As for timing, late spring is a great time to see juvenile sheep learning to play and run along the steep canyon walls. Late summer and fall is rutting time, when males bash horns to show dominance over one another and compete for the privilege of mating with one of the herd's eligible females.

While you'll need luck to see a bighorn sheep here today, chances are good if you linger long enough, you'll see another famous (albeit smaller) denizen of Yellowstone's Northern Range, the yellow-bellied marmot.

Below, from left: Yellow-bellied marmots love the rocky habitat of Sheepeater Cliff; if you have the patience, you'll definitely see one or more scurrying about.

Keep your eyes trained on Sheepeater Cliff for a few minutes until you see some movement—there's your marmot. He might signal his presence to you, and more importantly to his cohort, with a shrill short whistle. These reddish-brown and yellow rodents grow to about 2 feet long and 11 pounds and are closely related to (but bigger than) squirrels. Native to the northwestern United States and southwest Canada, their size and stored body fat help them make it through harsh northern winters, when they hibernate for up to eight months. Marmots typically live in colonies of ten to twenty animals in the rocky slopes of montane habitats, digging elaborate mazes of burrows. They feed twice a day on whatever grasses, flowers, insects, and even bird eggs that they can scrounge up nearby. Half the young marmots 'round these parts don't make it to their first birthdays thanks to coyotes, eagles, and other predators.

Bears, birds, and rodents love to eat the berries from the common juniper trees that pop up across just about every part of the high, dry American West, including right here in Yellowstone National Park.

◂ A closer view of the lichen-encrusted columnar basalt of Sheepeater Cliff.

Black willows crowd the edges of the Gardner River as it makes its way down toward Tukuarika Falls. ▸

While the view of Sheepeater Cliff may be what you came for, you'd be remiss not to wander down the unmarked trail that starts at the north end of the picnic area and follows the Gardner River downstream. The trail is mostly level but unmaintained: You'll have to pick your way over rocks and across fallen logs as you cut through thick riparian underbrush. Common juniper boughs stretch through the canopy, and black willow replaces big sagebrush as the dominant flora down closer to the river. Cameos by sticky geranium, wild strawberry, Canadian buffaloberry, and sticky cinquefoil lend some color pops to the otherwise green scene.

About .2 miles in, you'll see another columnar basalt cliff face strikingly similar to Sheepeater Cliff that also hosts a healthy yellow-bellied marmot colony. Within another half-mile you'll find Tukuarika Falls, where the Gardner River drops 25 feet through a narrow rock chute before bottoming into the middle of a lush riparian meadow. Your bird's-eye view from atop the cliff overlooking the river gives you a great overview of the ecosystem. Look for moose browsing the flats and trout rising up in the river on their way upstream.

The trail follows the clifftop for another few hundred feet, offering more opportunities to view the Gardner's riffles and chutes, before petering out entirely amidst overgrown willows. Retrace your steps, returning to Sheepeater Cliff and the picnic area, where you can sit and enjoy a bite of food before heading to your next destination.

THE HOODOOS

Giant boulders from an ancient landslide delight gawkers, climbers, and nature geeks

DIFFICULTY
Easy

LOCATION
North Yellowstone (Mammoth)

HIKE LENGTH
.25 mile

A jaunt into the Hoodoos gets prehistoric right quick. This *Flintstones*-esque setting features a jumbled assortment of uneven, white-rimmed boulders, many of them bigger than school buses and settled at odd angles across a 100-acre-plus swath of pristine Yellowstone high country.

Just a mile and a half south of Mammoth Hot Springs, access the Hoodoos via a small, unmarked pullout on the west side of the road. Explorers of all ages and abilities will enjoy walking, running, jumping, or even climbing here. Even those who prefer the car can enjoy the scenery.

The Hoodoos came to be when ancient Terrace Mountain, a collection of springs much like Mammoth Hot Springs today, built up and then went dormant. At some point later, an earthquake ripped through the region, sending huge rocks from Terrace Mountain's white-banded top layer crashing downhill to the southeast. Early explorers misnamed the resulting landscape feature "hoodoos," given the likeness to actual hoodoos—columns or pinnacles of weathered rock—found at other sites in the American Southwest, like at Bryce Canyon National Park. Yellowstone's Hoodoos are actually travertine limestone boulders scattered haphazardly by that seismic event.

Geologists haven't pinned down exactly when the earthquake that created Yellowstone's Hoodoos occurred, but they know it happened after the last ice age, so sometime in the past 15,000 years. The reasoning goes that if glaciers had passed this way, they would have scoured the landscape and moved the rocks along to new locations—so termed glacial erratics.

No doubt the rocks dominate the landscape here. Some of the whitish gray slabs have rounded edges, likely eroded over millennia, while others maintain long, straight edges as if they fell from Terrace Mountain just yesterday. Of course, these boulders all landed here at the same time, likely in one violent geological upsetting of the apple cart. But individual

‹ Yellowstone's Grand Loop Road passes right through the middle of the Hoodoos, not far from Mammoth Hot Springs.

Hundreds of boulders of all shapes and sizes make the Hoodoos a great stop for kids of all ages looking to stretch their legs, climb a rock, and take in epic views.

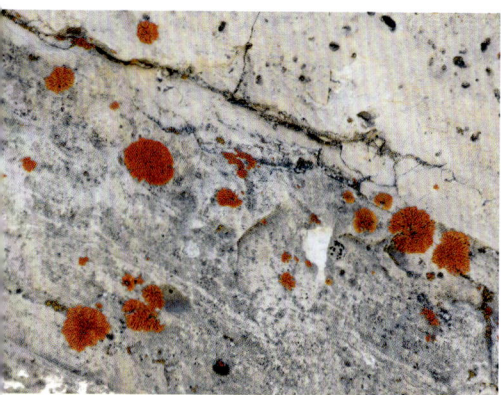

rocks landed in specific locations, at specific angles to the sun, making for microcosmic ecosystems on and around each and every one. The profusion of life, even in this forlorn rockpile of a landscape, is dazzling. Even the least hospitable of all of nature's surfaces—a rock face exposed to full sunlight, not to mention wind and precipitation—supports life in the form of lichens.

Seemingly simple yet utterly complex, these lifeforms are composed of two separate organisms, a fungus and an alga, working in tandem for mutual benefit. The fungus gives the lichen its shape and structure, providing protection for the alga, which collects and provides nutrients in a perfect symbiotic match. Here on the rock faces of the Hoodoos, brain-like Meruliaceae form ovals and circles of rusty ochre, while dark red Nectriaceae look like the center of a sunflower with textured dots.

It's a harsh, exposed setting here at 7300 feet elevation, and only the hardiest of flora hold their own in the predominantly rock-bound landscape. One of the best adapted is wax currant, which you'll see sprouting from cracks and gaps between boulders. These sometimes pungent shrubs—the hairs on their stems can smell like carrion—grow four-plus feet and spread much wider, depending on the habitat. Their highly veined, leathery green leaves fan out in three to five lobes with gently scalloped edges. In spring, currants bloom in pale yellow half-inch tubular flowers beloved by pollinators for their generous nectar stores. In late summer, the plants produce red-orange berries that birds and other animals gobble up.

Above, from left: Lichens like this Meruliaceae add dashes of color and texture to the otherwise white-gray rock faces of the Hoodoos.

Sticky cinquefoil is one of the hardy wildflowers hanging on for dear life within the Hoodoos' unfriendly jumble of boulders.

Above, from left:
Common juniper opportunistically fills in a crack between boulders.

Wax currant is one of several members of the gooseberry family that thrive in the dry, rocky soils of Yellowstone's Northern Range.

Another plant that thrives in the dry, rocky subalpine soils of the Hoodoos is common juniper. This conifer has the largest geographical range of any woody plant the world over, as far north as the Arctic circle and south to Texas. While it may survive in a range of habitats, common juniper is most at home in high, dry mid-latitude settings like much of Yellowstone National Park.

And while some become tree-like, junipers here tend to be spreaders, growing only three to five feet tall but reaching out far and wide. These hardy shrubs are intolerant of shade and do best in harsh environments where competition is minimal. It's not uncommon for them to live 100 years or longer in settings like this.

Junipers may rule the shrub layer here, but the dominant tree species at this harsh, exposed altitude is the subalpine fir. While these trees can grow to be 150 feet down at lower elevations, up here, 80 feet is about the most a young subalpine fir can aspire to. The only true firs in Yellowstone, subalpine firs have needles that sprout individually from branches, instead of in clusters. Their cones also grow upright on the branch, eventually drying in the wind and blowing away (other conifers drop their cones).

These trees' slender, spire-shaped form—that classic Christmas tree look—is an adaptation to living with heavy snows. Upper branches are too short to be weighed down and snapped, while longer, lower branches do support snow, but end up splayed and pressed to the ground in a wide radius around the trunk, eventually growing new roots where they meet the soil. This layering allows the tree to create

mats of branches from which new trees can sprout and grow, helping the species maintain and expand its territory.

That said, the warming of the high country thanks to climate change could potentially wreak havoc on subalpine fir populations, which can't move higher upslope—they are already at treeline. Meanwhile, other tree and plant species are moving uphill in response to warming, crowding into firs' traditional domain. This environmental double whammy of decreased habitat hospitality and increased competition for resources could relegate Yellowstone's subalpine firs to the history books.

Expect to see your fair share of animal activity if you're here at the edges of the day and spend time sitting and waiting. With so many perching spots and great cover beneath the giant boulders, birds nest and pass through the Hoodoos in abundance. If you're looking to add a Clark's nutcracker, Townsend's solitaire, northern flicker, red-breasted nuthatch, or mountain chickadee to your birding life list, you could be in luck here if you wait long enough. And raptors are especially fond of the perching opportunities and sightlines down into the crevices provided by the Hoodoos' unique geological structure.

• Subalpine fir trees thrive at this high elevation but face tough times ahead if climate change shrinks the species' available habitat.

Biologists worry that an uptick in energy development and supporting infrastructure across the Intermountain West in recent years could be bad for golden eagle populations. •

If you see an eagle-like bird gliding above but it doesn't have a white head, it's probably a golden eagle hunting rodents. These aerial predators look like their bald eagle cousins save for darker coloring: brown with golden feathers running down the backs of their heads and necks. They feed on a steady diet of small mammals but occasionally prey on elk calves, mule deer fawns, and even coyote pups. While golden eagles were never as common in North America as their more famous kin, their population also hasn't fluctuated as dramatically as other raptors, given their habitat and dietary preferences. Goldens gravitate to more remote, often inland, mountainous areas and don't tend to eat fish or other birds' eggs that can carry pesticides. That said, development across the American West is a threat to these raptors.

Speaking of prey, the Hoodoos play host to a variety of small mammals. All eight inches of the least chipmunk, with its signature black and white racing stripes from nose to tail and brown underbelly, dart around under logs and behind rocks just as soon as you can spot them.

Another frequently sighted mammal here is red squirrel. This foot-long brown-red squirrel zigzags around rock piles and cuts pinecones down from trees in fall to cache in middens for winter. Grizzly bears love to raid these middens when they find them, turning weeks of work by an industrious red squirrel into a light snack.

Listen for the shrill whistles of the American pika as it signals its exact whereabouts to other pikas—and warns of the nearby threat (you)—from various perches within the scree. These native lagomorphs (relatives of rabbits) average about eight inches long and five to six ounces, about the size of a guinea pig. They live off grasses, weeds, and wildflowers in spring and summer, drying extras in the sun. These leftovers get saved inside the pikas' dens and provide vital winter sustenance.

Pikas do not hibernate—in winter, they get around via tunnels they burrow in the snow. These gray-brown, round-eared cuties are exquisitely adapted to these alpine environments, blending into their surroundings so as to evade

‹ The American pika evolved in alpine environments and likes it best when temperatures hover around the freezing mark.

predation. But while vigilance is key to living out their six- to seven-year lifespan and avoid predation, the biggest threat facing the pika is global warming.

The lowly pika has become a symbol of the need to rein in emissions and stave off cataclysmic climate change, given rising temperatures in the (once) cool, moist alpine eco-systems they inhabit. Pikas evolved to prefer sub-freezing temperatures, and as the climate warms, they are forced to move to higher elevations. But there's less and less suitable habitat higher up the slopes, leaving pika essentially home-less and at greater risk. A pika can overheat and die when the mercury tops 78°F.

Researchers have found that pikas have disappeared from as much as a third of their previous range in the American West, and environmentalists are urging the federal gov-ernment to list the pika as an endangered species. Only time will tell whether this unassuming high-country mammal is afforded more protection from the warming effects of global climate change. Even if the pika does make it onto the endangered species list, it's hard to believe we'll rein in emissions soon enough to save it from extinction.

With no marked trails through the Hoodoos per se, enjoy a free-range wander at your own pace, but watch your step; without trails, you're more likely to sprain an ankle (or worse) if you're not careful. If you're feeling spry, pick an appropriate hoodoo, climb to the top, and drink in the 360-degree panoramic view. Cathedral Rock (elevation 7392 feet) adorns the landscape half a mile to the southeast, while another half-mile beyond that Bunsen Peak (elevation 8500 feet) features some interesting eroded rock spires on its near flank. Between here and there, look for evidence of glaciers passing this way at the end of the last ice age in the form of remnant glacial moraines—essentially, gravel depos-its left behind as the ice retreated. In the opposite direction, scope out the crumbling remains of old Terrace Mountain (elevation 8002 feet), about a mile northwest; further afield that direction are Clagett Butte (elevation 8041 feet) and Sepulcher Mountain (elevation 9633 feet).

When you've had enough of hoodoos and epic views, carefully retrace your steps to your car. You just might have to pinch yourself so you know your experience traversing this otherworldly landscape wasn't all a dream.

MAMMOTH HOT SPRINGS

White travertine terracing unfolds in a beautiful and otherworldly, desolate landscape

DIFFICULTY
Easy

LOCATION
North Yellowstone (Mammoth)

HIKE LENGTH
1.75 miles

I f you visit Yellowstone and don't spend some time checking out the constantly shifting travertine terraces of Mammoth Hot Springs, you'll have missed one of the park's most unique landscapes and perhaps its most dynamic geothermal area.

To access the elaborate 1.75-mile network of boardwalks traversing both the Upper and Lower terraces of Mammoth Hot Springs, drive 5.75 miles south from the park's North Entrance on the Grand Loop Road (Highway 89), passing the historic Mammoth Hot Springs Hotel (check out the map room if you're wandering) and the Albright Visitor Center (impressive displays and well-informed rangers) to a parking area on the road's

This travertine column on the edge of Mammoth Hot Springs was named "Liberty Cap" by the Hayden Survey of 1871 because it resembled the peaked knit caps worn by freedom fighters during the French Revolution. ▾

west side. You're greeted by Liberty Cap, a 40-foot tower of travertine left over by a long-extinct hot spring, which deposited layer after layer of minerals over hundreds of years before burning out.

Park here and head to the trails of the Lower Terraces. You'll see immediately what sets Mammoth Hot Springs

The Lower Terraces at Mammoth Hot Springs are covered in white travertine as well as streaks of sulfur. Note the standing dead lodgepole pines amidst the terraced hillside.

apart from geothermal areas elsewhere in the park. Old Faithful and the other features of the Upper Geyser Basin are based on alkaline-chloride chemistry, and Mud Volcano and the like are acid-sulfate-derived—but Mammoth's springs trade in calcium carbonate derived from the limestone underlay unique to this quadrant of the park.

Mammoth Hot Springs is fueled, so to speak, by a daily flush of some 750,000 gallons of superheated water from Norris Geyser Basin, about 20 miles south and just within the Yellowstone caldera. This hot water makes its way north via an elaborate network of natural plumbing. When it reaches Mammoth, it mixes with dissolved carbon dioxide and forms a solution of weak carbonic acid that dissolves calcium carbonate from the area's limestone underlay.

As this mixture precipitates (bubbles) out of thermal features here, it dries into the white travertine overlay you see before you. The travertine forms at the expense of carbonate rocks dissolving underground throughout Mammoth, which is how the landscape gets its terraced styling.

Compared to the sinter deposits found in nearby geothermal systems (Upper Geyser Basin, Norris Geyser Basin, etc.), which build up at a rate of 1 to 2 inches a year, the travertine that forms Mammoth's terraces rises at a rate of about 2 inches per week—although it doesn't last as long, given ever-shifting water flows below the surface that change where minerals precipitate.

It is a desolate landscape indeed. The fact that so much of the land is covered in chalky travertine gives the place a post-apocalyptic feel compared to acid-sulfur geothermal areas like Old Faithful.

Looping around on the footpath here, one of the first notable features you'll see is Palette Spring, which streams scalding water in orange and brown crisscrossing lines down over the little moguls it sits atop, while terraces further below have solidified in place as they oozed eons ago,

▲ Palette Spring feels like a place outside of time.

▲ You'll be in luck if you find colorful Canary Spring active.

giving it a weird, frozen-in-time vibe. The orange and brown coloration comes from Oscillatoria, a microbe that thrives in the medium-hot thermal environment at Mammoth.

If you continue counterclockwise around the Lower Terraces Loop, you'll encounter Minerva, Cleopatra, and Jupiter terraces, then on to Main Terrace, which is mostly white with yellow striations of sulfur coming from its vents. Sulfur is also the source of the rotten-egg smell so common around thermal features like these.

Next up is Canary Spring, a milky, light blue pool primarily covered in a chalky film of white travertine, save for a small eyeball-like center. Canary has sustained several periods of dormancy lasting months, years, and even decades, but it's active as of this writing.

Between the travertine terraces, don't be surprised by barren patches of ground that look like ghosts of grass and dirt; these areas were previously covered in travertine that has since moved on, killing all the plant matter below it in its wake. Likewise, you'll pass occasional lodgepole pine skeletons growing from travertine-covered land. These trees couldn't survive the mineral incursion into surrounding soils, but at least now the dead snags provide valuable perching and nesting habitat for a range of insects and birds.

Speaking of birds, some of the avian species seen around Mammoth include yellow-rumped warbler, black-billed magpie, gray jay, and red-naped sapsucker. Aside from birds, Rocky Mountain elk and American bison occasionally wander through, but the fragile travertine terraces aren't particularly friendly for these animals to walk on—occasionally one falls to its death—so they tend to stick to more stable terrain.

Another wildlife species that isn't native to these parts and threatens to wreak havoc around Mammoth is the mountain goat. These sure-footed, rock-hopping, white-bearded ungulates wouldn't be here in Yellowstone had hunters not introduced small numbers into the nearby Absaroka and Madison mountain ranges in the 1940s. Some of these animals migrated into the park to head up new family groups. For the last few decades, these black-horned goats have chomped up native plants and forage of bighorn sheep and other Yellowstone wildlife. Biologists continue to debate what, if anything, to do about these rogue goats roaming the Northern Range.

Follow the path uphill to the Upper Terrace boardwalks and sites (or take the driving route described below): Prospect Terrace, New Highland Terrace, Orange Spring Mound, Bath Lake, White Elephant Back Terrace, and Angel Terrace. At this point, you have a good sense of what makes Mammoth tick—follow the loop back around down through the Lower Terraces to your car near Liberty Cap.

Above, from left:
Red-naped sapsuckers make themselves at home drilling into the wood of standing dead lodgepole pines at Mammoth.

Mountain goats are not native to Yellowstone but are thriving nevertheless, affecting food supplies of foragers like bighorn sheep, bison, elk, and deer.

Alternatively, you can drive the perimeter of the Upper Terrace on Upper Terrace Road, a one-lane, one-way one-and-a-half mile loop road with pullouts so you can hop out of the car and onto a boardwalk for a closer look. You can even leave your car at a roadside pullout along Upper Terrace Road and walk down into the Lower Terraces from there.

However you experience Mammoth Hot Springs, you'll leave with a newfound appreciation for the variety of geothermal features on offer at Yellowstone, and for the power of Mother Nature in creating ephemeral landscapes that are worthy works of art in and of themselves.

WRAITH FALLS

An 80-foot waterfall sluices through
wildflower-festooned mixed forest

DIFFICULTY
Easy

LOCATION
North Yellowstone (Mammoth)

HIKE LENGTH
1 mile

This short hike skirts a verdant meadow before crossing through Douglas fir forest and over a small creek to a lookout across to lovely Wraith Falls. The fact these different landforms occur across just a half-mile underscores what makes Yellowstone so great: you don't have to go far to see amazing sights and learn about nature's workings.

Park at the well-marked pullout for Wraith Falls on the south side of the Grand Loop Road five miles east-southeast of Mammoth Hot Springs. The parking area only fits about a dozen cars, but the hike is short enough that plenty come and go at regular intervals; if you wait around long enough, a spot will open up.

The trail starts right there, heading south through a meadow dominated by mountain big sagebrush mixing it up with common juniper and scattered Douglas fir trees growing next to glacial erratic nurse rocks—that is, boulders that provide shade, moisture, and protection to the lucky tree seeds that find their way there and can flourish.

In spring or summer, expect to see lots of wildflowers here in the meadow. Sulfur cinquefoil sparkles trailside with its spiny, off-white blooms. Sticky geranium's flowers sport an intricate veined purple-and-white star formation. Shrubby cinquefoil adds some yellow flair to the scene. The densely clustered purplish-baby-blue corollas of small-flowered penstemon, common along the trail at this elevation, radiate out from central cores, beckoning bees for a little pollination initiation.

Meanwhile, elegant Wasatch penstemon features a mid-blue to violet-purple gradient from the tip to the base of its tubular petals. Silky lupine, seemingly ubiquitous around Yellowstone, occupies a similar color palette and provides bees with a lot of bang for the pollination buck while helping to enrich surrounding soil through its ability to fix nitrogen.

Arrowleaf balsamroot's perky yellow flowers in groupings of six make humans smile and attract many moths, butterflies, and bees, which come for nectar and leave covered in pollen. Rocky mountain elk, bighorn sheep, and mule deer feed extensively on this plant's nourishing shoots and flowers, while deer mice and Uinta ground squirrels eat and

‹ A sagebrush-dominated meadow gives way to the mixed forest that cloaks Wraith Falls.

sometimes cache its nutritious seeds. Prior to white settlement, Indigenous tribes across the region used salves and teas made from the locally widespread plant to treat a range of maladies from body aches, bruises, and insect bites to fevers, whooping cough, and even tuberculosis.

Fireweed pokes up its wrinkly magenta flowers with yellow stigmas from clearings large and small. This prolific plant grows both rhizomatically and through wind-dispersed seeds, earning its nickname by quickly colonizing burned-over forest in the earliest stage of so-called forest succession. Hillsides across Yellowstone were painted magenta in the spring of 1989, after massive wildfires rolled through the park the previous summer.

Woods' rose shows off its pink blooms in spring and early summer, and as fall approaches, offers up its nutritious hips (berries) beloved by bears as well as songbirds like the Bohemian waxwing and Townsend's solitaire. And lucky hikers won't be able to resist popping back a few wild red raspberries that have ripened along the trail.

Another flowering plant you'll likely encounter trailside, much to the chagrin of park biologists, is houndstongue. This invasive plant's dark violet-colored flowers produce large numbers of pollen grains that easily attach to the coats of passing animals, distributing themselves around the park and beyond. This dread species probably came here in seed form within hay used by both the National Park Service and guided horseback riding concessionaires. Park Service biologists are keeping their eyes on this and dozens of other invasive plant species on the march within Yellowstone.

▲ A few of the wildflowers you may see along the Wraith Falls Trail include shrubby cinquefoil, sticky geranium, and small-flowered penstemon.

Above, from left: Houndstongue is among dozens of invasive plant species worrying park biologists.

The trail to Wraith Falls leads through a refreshing mixed forest dominated by Engelmann spruce trees.

In a few hundred feet, the trail turns into a boardwalk over a marshier stretch before crossing tiny Lupine Creek on a small wooden footbridge and entering the forest. While most of Yellowstone's forests are dominated by densely packed lodgepole pines, here a more diverse mix of trees provides an airier setting with more room between trees and different types of branches and boughs swooping down at odd angles. Douglas fir dots the periphery of the woods, and as you hike deeper in, Engelmann spruce takes over, eventually cloaking the trail in a veritable robe of deep green.

Soon enough, you'll start the only real ascent to speak of on this hike, gaining about 50 feet in elevation around one switchback. Dwarf huckleberry also lines both sides of the trail here; if it's late summer or early fall, help yourself to the delicious blue-black fruits that are like tart blueberries—if a bear hasn't already beaten you to them all. (As always, when hiking in Yellowstone, watch out for bears and have bear spray at the ready.)

In another 200 feet, the trail dead-ends at a small aerie overlook protected by a wooden railing and a view directly across to Wraith Falls on the other side of a small ravine. The falls make their 80-foot drop over a huge, bulbous boulder that divides cascading Lupine Creek into two streams that essentially rejoin at the bottom and follow this ravine. The glassy, apparitional nature of this unique waterfall reminded members of the Hague expedition of 1885 of a "wraith" (ghost), and the name obviously stuck.

Scan the earthen hillside across the ravine and to the sides of Wraith Falls for signs of movement. A small colony of yellow-bellied marmots that call this rocky cliffside home

‹ Lupine Creek drains off the Blacktail Deer Plateau over ghostly Wraith Falls before trailing downstream in the ravine below.

are often out whistling and cavorting, though always keeping an eye out for marauding predators like coyotes or golden eagles. During summer, marmots fatten up on grasses, flowers, and insects in preparation for the long Yellowstone winter, when they spend eight months underground in hibernation.

Although Wraith Falls (and marmot machinations nearby) sure can be mesmerizing, do the hikers behind you a favor and don't overstay your welcome. While Wraith Falls may not be the most secluded destination in Yellowstone, it is inarguably easy to hike and convenient to the Grand Loop Road.

Make your way back the way you came, and see if you notice any different plants (or animals) on your return trip that you didn't see on your way in. Indeed, it's hard to believe the bounty of natural treasures on such a short, easy foray into the woods of Northwest Yellowstone.

FORCES OF THE NORTHERN RANGE

Boardwalk trail through a quintessential Northern Range ecosystem

DIFFICULTY
Easy

HIKE LENGTH
.5 mile

LOCATION
North Yellowstone (between Mammoth and Tower-Roosevelt)

A short boardwalk hike through open meadows and emerging stands of quaking aspen introduces visitors to the ecology of Yellowstone's Northern Range, a unique lower-elevation section of the national park that is a haven for wildlife. The combination of accessibility for visitors with disabilities, interpretive signage, and immersion in the environment means anyone who can walk or roll can enjoy the experience and learn something about nature and the interaction of species along the way.

Park at the well-marked pullout on the northern stretch of the Grand Loop Road (8.5 miles east of Mammoth Hot Springs or 10 miles west of Tower Junction, depending on which direction you're coming from). Two-dozen-plus cars could squeeze in here, but you'll rarely have much company. Head north on the boardwalk.

As you immerse yourself in the landscape, you'll notice how much drier it seems than other high-elevation, mostly forested sections of the park. In this xeric (dry) environment, Wyoming big sagebrush dominates on both sides of the boardwalk and as far as you can see in every direction. Bluebunch wheatgrass and Sandberg bluegrass fill in the gaps. In mesic (not overly dry or wet) sections of the Northern Range, Idaho fescue and Columbia needlegrass are players as well.

During warmer months, periodic wildflower blooms punctuate the landscape with dashes of color. Starting in May, look for big, pointy, radiating yellow blooms of arrowleaf balsamroot, standing 2 feet tall in groups of eight to twelve flowers. Late spring also finds nodding, seed-filled pink-red blossoms of prairie smoke, its flower tufts flapping in the breeze so spring winds can easily disperse its seeds. Even later in spring, larkspur sends out little shelves (or spurs) under its purple-blue, bird's-head-shaped blooms to tempt pollinators to perch, while wild flax bursts forth in light purple-pink, five-lobed flowers with yellow stamens. Heartleaf arnica, yellow violet, sticky geranium, Rocky Mountain phlox, lance-leaved stonecrop, and silky lupine are a few others in the Northern Range wildflower parade.

The environment here on Yellowstone's so-called Northern Range is markedly different from most of the rest of the park, given its lower elevation and precipitation. This combination and the abundance of forage makes this 600-square-mile swath ideal winter habitat for grazing animals frustrated by deeper snows at higher elevations. The profusion of grazers—including Yellowstone's biggest herd of Rocky Mountain elk as well as American bison, mule deer, bighorn sheep, and pronghorn—draws many predators, like gray wolves, grizzly bears, and coyotes. It's

The rolling hills around the Forces of the Northern Range Trail are underlaid by welded tuff, a form of volcanic ash compressed by time and the elements into solid rock. ▾

an ecological win-win: There is plenty of grass for the herbivores and plenty of meat for the carnivores.

Look out for the rocky outcrop due west that reveals something of the region's volcanic history. The Yellowstone supervolcano first exploded some 2 million years ago, coating the landscape with ash for thousands of miles around. Near the site of the explosion, deep layers of ash compressed (or welded) over the eons into the rocks in front of us today. This type of rock, dubbed Huckleberry Ridge Tuff by geologists, is visible in outcroppings throughout the Northern Range. Not only do these scattered outcrops lend variety to the otherwise flat landscape, they also provide habitat for a range of small mammals, birds, and insects.

After about 250 feet, if you go right at the junction, soon you'll find a side trail to the right (east) that leads to a resting spot where the boardwalk encircles a stand of young quaking aspen trees. While aspens aren't at all out of place, their absence has been conspicuous here for the better part of the last century, and their return is part of a larger conservation success story.

The virtual absence of aspens, willows, and cottonwoods across the Northern Range for about a century following park establishment was due to overgrazing by elk and other ungulates after white pioneers and traders extirpated gray wolves (and decimated populations of other predators) in an effort to make Yellowstone a better place to visit, as settlers had done across the West.

With their natural predators no longer on the scene, elk populations irrupted (increased suddenly). Biologists

Wyoming big sagebrush is the dominant groundcover across the sagebrush-steppe ecosystem of Yellowstone's Northern Range.

estimate as many as 30,000 elk may have attempted to overwinter in the Northern Range; unsurprisingly, the hungry animals ate themselves out of house and home. Willow, cottonwood, and aspen trees were eaten twig by twig over the course of harsh winters, and new shoots, tastiest of all, were snarfed down long before they could gain a foothold. Wyoming big sagebrush, a low-quality browse, was the only forage available, and even that became scarce. At the other end of the pendulum swing of an unbalanced ecosystem, elk starved to death, their population plummeting. This irruption cycle repeated itself several times during the 20th century.

Reintroduction of gray wolves back into Yellowstone in 1995 ushered in a new era of so-called natural regulation, whereby ecosystem dynamics dictate how many elk can support how many wolves based on available habitat, with populations settling accordingly. Wildlife managers let nature run its course instead of selectively thinning or relocating elk from the Yellowstone herd. Elk numbers here declined from nearly 20,000 in 1995, the year wolves were reintroduced, to around 6000 today.

Just about everyone agrees the reintroduction of wolves has been an overwhelming success in ecological restoration. This healthy young stand of aspen is a great reminder.

Retrace your steps back to the main loop and turn right to continue on the path counterclockwise, S-curving through a dense stand of lodgepole pines to another lookout with views through the trees to the east.

The next stop along the boardwalk delivers you to another short side trail that dead-ends in another circle,

Above, from left:
Quaking aspen leaves shimmer in the late afternoon light.

A lodgepole pine produces pollen in its catkins every spring.

Glaciers dislodged boulders from mountainsides and carried them dozens or even hundreds of miles before melting and dumping them willy-nilly upon the landscape. ▸

this time around a solitary glacial erratic boulder. This car-sized granite hunk was likely wedged from a mountain in the Absaroka Range 30 miles east by a glacier, which transported it here before melting at the end of the last ice age 10,000 years ago.

Looking out across the flats, you'll notice lots of others, smaller, but just as erratically placed. Covering almost every inch of these boulders are flat, light-green and black *Lecanora muralis* lichens, which radiate out in big spots and splotches—their Latin-derived epithet *muralis* means "growing on the wall." Like all lichens, *Lecanora muralis* is a compound organism composed of an alga (which

◂ The sun sets on Yellowstone's verdant Northern Range.

provides energy through photosynthesis) and a fungus (which provides structure and protection). It's not hard to believe lichens are one of the most widespread organisms on the planet when they spread out on almost every available substrate in this place of weather extremes. Biologists have identified some 3600 different lichens across North America; ten percent of them can be found in Yellowstone.

Back on the main boardwalk, follow the curve south and to a viewpoint with a panoramic perspective on sagebrush steppe transitioning to lodgepole forest transitioning to the snow-capped peaks of the Gallatin Range breaking through the western horizon. These wide-open sightlines make you realize why this area is so great for grazing: elk and other ruminants can see threats coming from miles away across the flat expanse of steppe.

After taking in this panorama and returning to the main loop, it's another 350 feet to the junction where the lollipop began, and then a hop, skip, and a jump back to the trailhead and parking area. While Forces of the Northern Range may not be as wild as many of Yellowstone's short hiking trails, it provides visitors ample information on the landscape before them and the wild inhabitants who live there. You won't soon forget your time walking this boardwalk, and what you'll have learned will be sure to enrich the rest of your Yellowstone experience.

PETRIFIED TREE

An ancient petrified redwood tree offers a glimpse of a milder climate in the distant past

DIFFICULTY
Easy

HIKE LENGTH
.1 mile

LOCATION
North Yellowstone (Tower-Roosevelt)

W hile it's hard to believe the climate around Yellowstone was wet and warm at one point in geological history, a petrified redwood tree relic on a Northern Range hillside here confirms it.

Find the turnoff for Petrified Tree off the northern section of Yellowstone's Grand Loop Road, 1.3 miles west of Tower Junction. Follow this paved road a half mile to its terminus. (Trailers and RVs can park in a small turnaround right near the turnoff and walk a quarter mile to the tree— only cars should drive to the end, given the tight turning radius required to exit.)

Find the paved path across from the parking spots and follow it 300 feet, where it deposits you at the doorstep of the massive, 50 million-year-old petrified redwood. If you were hoping to reach out and touch some petrified rock, sorry—you're a century too late. Rock hounds cleared away two petrified redwood remnants nearby before park officials put up a wrought-iron fence surrounding this last tree in the early 1900s. Today, a modern facsimile of this fencing still stands.

Contrary to popular belief, this petrified trunk didn't actually grow here, even though it is standing up

Petrified by exposure to volcanic silica 50 million years ago, this coast redwood is now a stone relic of an epoch long past. ▾

in the soil as if it did. In fact, the tree has no roots and still stands only because it's propped up around its base by millennia's worth of sediment buildup.

Prior to 1980, everyone assumed the tree had grown here, but the aha moment came following the eruption of Mt. St. Helens in Washington State, when researchers there noticed uprooted trees floating in Spirit Lake at the volcano's base becoming waterlogged and sinking vertically, lodging themselves in quickly building layers of ash and sediment that raised the floor of the lakebed. These "upright floaters" came into the scene at intervals, embedding in successive sedimentary layers.

▲ A sign outside of the Petrified Tree's fence makes it clear that prospecting for pieces of petrified wood on the surrounding hillside is not allowed.

This petrified redwood trunk got here in just the same manner. It was torn off at its roots, most likely through volcanic trauma, in the Eocene epoch and ended up floating in the huge lake covering the region at the time. As the trunk took on water, it sank vertically, dragged down by the rocks and other debris bound up in the root remnants of its lower trunk, and embedded upright in settling waves of sediments. Remnants of other petrified trees are present up and down the hillside—in different sedimentary layers of what was formerly the lakebed—surrounding the fenced-off relic (but good luck finding any aboveground nowadays, as the hillside has been picked clean by rock hunters). Trees here and nearby, including at Specimen Ridge, were buried as such in these rolling mixes of volcanic silica, ash, and water. Before these trees could rot, flowing silica would plug up their living cells, petrifying them for time immemorial by turning what was porous wood into stone.

Anatomically identical to the coast redwoods of modern-day California save for its petrified state and shorn-off roots, this age-old trunk indicates the environment around these parts was much warmer, damper, and more violent tens of millions of years in the rearview mirror.

The fact the surrounding landscape is today's typical Yellowstone environment—colder and significantly drier than can support redwoods—makes the presence of such a tree here odder still.

The living plants seen here that fit right in include parsnipflower buckwheat and giant wildrye. Uphill at a distance, Rocky Mountain Douglas firs thrive in the moist upland soils that provide more nutritional support than much of the rest of Yellowstone.

Another plant creeping up around the Petrified Tree that park biologists are less enamored of is Dalmatian toadflax. This invasive plant with spry green stalks topped with clusters of horn-shaped yellow flowers is native to Mediterranean Europe. It was introduced in the United States long ago as a decorative garden ornamental but quickly jumped the fence and spread like the weed it is here in the virgin territory of the so-called New World. It has been a floral pest in Yellowstone since the 1960s, when initial efforts to eradicate it from the park with biological and chemical controls proved futile. Indeed, Dalmatian toadflax and its equally invasive cousin yellow toadflax remain of great concern to park biologists, as they spread quickly and disrupt local plant and animal communities.

Elk, bison, bighorn sheep, mule deer, and pronghorn steer clear of toadflax, as it's too hard to digest and provides little nutrition. If it displaces native plants ungulates are accustomed to, who knows its effects on prey and predator populations? What's more troubling is Dalmatian toadflax and yellow toadflax are only a couple of the 225 or so non-native plants worrying biologists at Yellowstone these days. The incursion of non-natives is inevitable, but nonetheless, biologists are working hard preventing the spread of some three dozen noxious invasive plants here in the park.

But don't get hung up on the battle against invasive species when

Dalmatian toadflax, a native of Europe, was introduced to the United States long ago as a garden ornamental. It became an invasive species in the Intermountain West, where it can displace native forage and alter the predator/prey population balance of an entire region. ▾

you've got a 50-million-year-old fish-out-of-water redwood to contemplate. Will it still be here 50 million years in the future? What manmade objects will also be here to tell of humanity's influence on the planet? Only time will tell.

When your visiting hour is over at the side of the Petrified Tree, make your way back, content in having just time-traveled 50 million years into the past to a dramatically different ecosystem right in this very spot. Mother Nature, in all her varied forms, is amazing indeed!

▲ It's hard to believe this tree didn't grow here, but alas, its shorn roots belowground prove it was ripped up elsewhere and deposited here.

YELLOWSTONE RIVER PICNIC AREA

Sagebrush and stellar views on the east rim of the Narrows of the Yellowstone River

DIFFICULTY
Easy to
Moderate

HIKE LENGTH
.5 to 2 miles

LOCATION
Northeast Yellowstone (Tower-Roosevelt)

Immerse yourself in the high and wild world on a knife-edge trail along the eastern rim of the Narrows of the Yellowstone River, with hundred-mile views in every direction and a unique perspective looking down into the raging river canyon 300 feet below.

The hike starts out from a small picnic area off Highway 212 (also known as the Northeast Entrance Road), about 1.25 miles east of Tower Junction. It's a great stop for a picnic or leg stretch before or after a drive through the Lamar Valley to the east. The little wooded picnic area is tucked into the trees just off the road and features several tables and accompanying parking spots. If you're there to hike rather than linger, circle the loop to near its end and park in one of the few spots right by the trailhead proper. The well-marked trail starts there, by the south side of the loop.

Start out climbing on the trail as it skirts and then mounts the ridge, gaining 200 feet in elevation in this first quarter-mile ascent. As you move up through sagebrush-dominated landscape, you'll pass an assortment of gnarled, twisted Rocky Mountain Douglas fir trees and

Arrowleaf balsamroot, here backed by verdant mountain big sagebrush, is one of the more common wildflowers that blooms in early summer in Yellowstone National Park.

Clockwise from above: Hikers get up above the Narrows of the Yellowstone River on the ridgeline of the Yellowstone River Picnic Area Trail.

Rocky Mountain penstemon is more common further south but makes an occasional cameo here in the north country, especially in high, dry settings like this one.

A glacial erratic boulder, deposited here by a melting glacier 13,000 years ago, surrounded by mountain big sagebrush.

big boulders dropped by glaciers that melted at the end of the last Ice Age, 13,000 years ago. Before this spectacular thaw, the entire Yellowstone Caldera was buried under roughly 4000 feet of ice, including the spot where you are standing.

Boulders would chip off of nearby mountainsides, land atop glacial ice, and ride slowly for years over untold distances until things warmed up. These glacial erratic rocks were then dropped where the ice underneath finally melted away as the climate returned to something more akin to what we know today.

Here on the hillside near Yellowstone River Picnic Area, many of these glacial erratics serve as nurse rocks for the now huge, old Rocky Mountain Douglas fir trees growing from underneath them. These rocks earned that moniker because they provide protection from the elements for tree seeds looking for a shady, protected spot to take root. Just about all of the Douglas firs within immediate view here sprouted alongside a boulder. As you approach the top of the rise, look for an especially big Douglas fir that has literally split its massive, 70-something-foot-tall nurse rock in two by levering itself into a fissure in the granite.

THE PINEDALE GLACIATION

The two major Ice Ages that have had significant effects on the landforms around Yellowstone are the Bull Lake Glaciation, which occurred from about 150,000 to 130,000 years ago, and the much more recent Pinedale Glaciation, from 22,000 to 13,000 years ago. In present terms, the massive, ancient Bull Lake Glaciation extended from points south of the town of Jackson Hole to Yellowstone National Park's western border—or it might have been much larger, because evidence may have been altered or obliterated by more recent volcanism and glaciation. In any case, these ancient glaciers dammed local rivers and left behind piles of jumbled rock called moraines, which geologists can still identify today, despite the lapse of 130-plus millennia. Landscape analysis shows that major volcanic eruptions came before, during, and after the 20,000-year stretch when Yellowstone was buried under Bull Lake ice.

It's evidence of the newer Pinedale Glaciation that even laypeople can see all around Greater Yellowstone. During Pinedale's peak, an icecap some 4000 feet thick covered nearly the entire area. The terrain of the Lamar Valley was shaped extensively by catastrophic floods unleashed by the melt of ice dams that had blocked ancient waterways across what is

▴ It's hard to believe an ice cap filled in the gorge below and topped it by thousands more feet, eventually melting and dropping off boulders like these, now nurse rocks for Douglas firs here above the Narrows.

today Yellowstone's Northern Range. Pinedale glaciers are also responsible for the rolling topography of the Hayden Valley, as well as the fjord-like arms of Yellowstone Lake. Part of the reason the effects of the Pinedale glaciation are still visible is that no lava flows came afterward to wipe them away from the geological record.

Since the last big melt around 13,000 years ago, much of the ground around affected areas has risen several feet due to a phenomenon called uplift or unloading. The land itself, finally unburdened from the weight of tons of ice above it, actually rebounded to where it probably stood before the big Pinedale freeze. This type of rebounding is still going on to some extent in Greenland and Scandinavia, but geologists think it likely stopped in Greater Yellowstone a few thousand years ago.

Did the geothermal features so important in Yellowstone today play a role in melting or reducing the amount of ice covering the landscape back then?

The answer is a resounding no. Thanks to recent computer modeling, we know the thermal output from the geyser basins would only have melted about a foot of ice per year—a veritable drop in the bucket.

With its erupting volcanoes, gushing geysers, and steaming fumaroles—not to mention the occasional apocalyptic wildfire—Yellowstone may be known as the original land of fire, but we can't forget that ice has been a big player in shaping the landscapes and ecology of the region.

Soon enough you'll crest the ridge. Take in the priceless panorama here for as long as you like—on a clear day, the sightlines seem endless. When you're done scouring every far horizon, peer down the steep cliffs below you into the so-called Narrows of the Yellowstone River, the narrowest section of the river's run. The roaring whitewater some 300 feet down is hurtling toward the Grand Canyon of the Yellowstone, 18 river miles to the south.

Spreading phlox is among dozens of summertime wildflowers you'll see while hiking the rim of the Narrows. ▾

From the top here, the narrow knife-edge footpath continues to the left (south), traversing the ridgeline. Sprigs of sagebrush dominate the trailside but occasionally give way to clusters of arrowleaf balsamroot, with its big, floppy yellow flowers in early summer. Silky lupine adds dashes of purple-blue to the otherwise drab landscape palette. The small, white five-petaled stars of spreading phlox punctuate occasional patches with little clusters of asterisks. Meanwhile, Rocky Mountain penstemons look like tricolored butterflies dressed in blue, purple, and white.

Only a few trees hang on up here—Douglas fir, Engelmann spruce, Rocky Mountain junipers, and the occasional lodgepole pine—and they are trained by the wind and snow-

fall into twisted, stunted shapes. One particular husk of a Douglas fir, singed to the core by a lightning strike but still standing in a blackened visage of its former self, stands sentinel over the hillside, warning you to head for lower ground if electric storms are coming your way.

As for wildlife, American bison are often roaming around up here; keep your distance if you see any of these primordial one-ton ungulates. Likewise, there is a lot to like here for both black and grizzly bears, so stay alert, hike in groups of at least two, and make some noise as you go. Bighorn sheep, pronghorn, and mule deer also frequent this liminal ridgeline strip, foraging on its relative abundance of good eats. Look for osprey perched in the cliffs across the river; there's some great

From top: You might see bison out on the ridge above the Yellowstone River, but you'll definitely see some bison dung. This natural fertilizer serves as food for the plants of this range.

A burned out Douglas fir snag warns hikers to seek lower ground and take cover in case of lightning strikes nearby.

fishing for them as Yellowstone cutthroat trout run the rapids below.

At about a mile in, look for puffs of steam rising from the rhyolite butte across the way known as Calcite Springs, where precipitating minerals have colored the cliffs in a chalky white film from their tip-tops right down to the water line hundreds of feet below. This makes a good turn-around point for those looking for a short jaunt. If that's you, retrace your steps to the picnic area and revel in how the views change when you see them from the opposite direction. You'll have covered about 2 miles out-and-back.

If a little extra hiking (totalling 3.9 miles) would do you well, continue south and then east as the trail follows the course of the river, affording views of the columnar basalt layers of Overhanging Cliff, rock pinnacles surrounding Tower Falls (the waterfall itself isn't visible from this angle), and historic Bannock Ford, a common crossing spot for Indigenous peoples in the region prior to white settlement. Soon enough you'll reach a junction with the Specimen Ridge Trail; follow it left (north), and eventually you'll be back at the Grand Loop Road. You can complete the loop by walking north along the roadside for three quarters of a mile to your parking spot at the Picnic area.

Whether you take the longer loop route or the shorter out-and-back option, you'll have filled your lungs with fresh air and taken in some of the most wondrous scenery in the Lower 48, and likely some iconic Yellowstone wildlife along the way.

‹ Silky lupine flowers are backed by a copse of Engelmann spruce high on the ridge above the Narrows of the Yellowstone River.

LAMAR VALLEY

Scenic drive through America's Serengeti with sweeping views and lots of bison

DIFFICULTY
Easy

DRIVE LENGTH
17 miles

LOCATION
Northeast Yellowstone (Tower-Roosevelt)

I f seeing wildlife amidst panoramic alpine vistas is part of Yellowstone's attraction for you, don't miss the Lamar Valley—America's Serengeti—in the northeast corner of the park. The beauty of driving the roughly 17-mile stretch of Highway 212 through Lamar Valley is that you can pull out at any number of spots along the way to stretch your legs and get better views, but you can also stay in the car (for protection) in case any bison or other wildlife are close by.

From the Grand Loop Road, head northeast on Highway 212 from Tower Junction. In .75 miles, the road crosses the Yellowstone River on a small bridge, and in another half mile, you'll be at the Yellowstone River Picnic Area, a sweet, shady spot with parking and picnic tables. This is also the jumping-off point for a short but dramatic hike up along the ridge above the river, the subject of another chapter in this book.

Continue on Highway 212 as it heads east and the verdant, forest-edged valley begins to take center stage. When you see an enticing pullout, park and get out to survey the scene as the Lamar's grasslands spread out to mountain flanks, all under a seemingly endless sky.

Lodgepole pines stick together at the edge of the Lamar Valley. ▾

Down in the valley below, mountain big sagebrush is widespread, along with cheatgrass, an invasive plant wreaking havoc across sagebrush steppe in the Intermountain West. While these two plants aren't favored by the elk, bison, moose, and deer that frequent the Lamar Valley, a wide range of others make for better forage for ungulates. Water sedge, beaked sedge, Nebraska sedge, horsetail, wire rush, sweetgrass, timothy, and tufted hairgrass are among the most common herbaceous delicacies here as far as elk and bison are concerned, but small-wing sedge, Raynold's sedge, white-scale sedge, Idaho fescue, Kentucky bluegrass, Columbia needlegrass, mountain brome, and giant wild-rye, among others, also make appearances.

Wildflowers interrupt the 1000 shades of green with outbursts of color. Cutleaf anemone sports pretty white and yellow flowers, while purple milkvetch sends up blooms that look like silky violet fingers coming out of hairy green knuckles gripping a tennis ball. Little larkspur's big floppy blooms look like flaccid purple stars, while daisies such as shaggy fleabane and slender fleabane pop up in all their ragged glory.

Glacial erratic boulders of various sizes are strewn randomly around the valley. You'll notice some acting as nurse rocks for solitary Douglas fir trees. There isn't a lot of cover on this glacially scoured valley bottom, so the shade of these boulders is one of the best spots to take root. The scattering of trees these rocks enable is increasing the boundary zone between the meadowy valley floor and upland forest surrounding it, thus increasing overall biodiversity by creating habitat niches quickly filled by a range of insects, rodents, and birds, among others.

Further uphill, dense stands of Douglas fir are a reminder the Lamar Valley is one of the few regions of Yellowstone where lodgepole pines are not the dominant tree species. This area is slightly lower in elevation, gets more precipitation, and holds more moisture in its soils than higher, drier landscapes where lodgepole reigns—perfect conditions for Douglas fir.

While these Rocky Mountain variants of the Douglas fir don't get as big as their cousins in the temperate rainforests of Washington and Oregon, they do typically top 100 feet, with diameters maxing out just north of 3 feet. These "Doug firs" can live up to 1200 years, though half that is probably closer to average. Part of what gives them their longevity is thick, furrowed bark that withstands the torment of all but the most rapacious of wildfires. If you see dark scarring around the base of one of these trees' trunks, you'll know it survived at least one major burn in the past.

Given what a big player Douglas fir is across the American West, it's no surprise it's much loved by a variety of species. Rocky Mountain elk browse its needles in late winter and early spring when other forage isn't yet available, sometimes topping trees so excessively that they develop curving, sideways boughs instead of the tall, straight trunks we normally associate with such conifers.

Meanwhile, red squirrels, deer mice, other rodents, and sometimes even birds eat large numbers of Douglas fir seeds from the forest floor, caching extras for winter. A

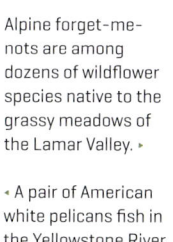

Alpine forget-me-nots are among dozens of wildflower species native to the grassy meadows of the Lamar Valley. ▸

◂ A pair of American white pelicans fish in the Yellowstone River.

range of songbirds—including Clark's nutcracker, mountain chickadee, red crossbill, and pine siskin—eat seeds right from Douglas fir cones. Hairy woodpeckers mine the trees' furrowed bark for insects and larvae, and dusky grouse rely on its needles and buds for winter sustenance.

Insect pests have been an issue for Douglas fir here over the years. Western spruce budworm, wooly aphid, and Douglas fir beetle have each had their way with some stands in recent decades, but all have declined to endemic levels among the hearty trees of late, so park biologists aren't overly worried about overall population health. That said, warming temperatures will likely invite new insect pests to these environs, and no one knows whether these Douglas firs, let alone other flora and fauna in the Lamar Valley, will be able to tolerate such new incursions.

Once you've marveled at the scene, continue east. About 4 miles further, the road crosses the Lamar River on a small bridge, then follows the watercourse closely for another 8 miles before turning northeast to parallel Soda Butte Creek.

As you drive, feel free to stop at any of the several pull-outs or wide shoulders along this main stretch if you see wildlife or any other sights worth a closer, more stationary

Get ready for a nonstop parade of bison in the Lamar Valley. ▾

examination. One viewpoint isn't necessarily better than another, but those where other cars are pulled over are a good bet for seeing wildlife, as that's likely why everyone else has stopped there. At some pullouts you'll discover little side trails up roadside embankments or down into meadows below.

As you make your way through Lamar Valley, don't be surprised if the tune of "Where the Buffalo Roam" buzzes through your head, as herds of American bison (aka buffalo) dozens strong are likely grazing on the range in front of you. Indeed, three-quarters of the park's estimated 5000 total bison live year-round in the Lamar Valley. (Most of the rest are in Hayden Valley to the south.)

The fact so many bison live here now is a conservation success story. Prior to white settlement, some 60 million bison roamed North America, but by 1900, only 300 animals were left across the continent, 23 of them in Yellowstone. In 1902, the US Army (which was in charge of Yellowstone between 1886 and 1916, when the National Park Service was created) set up the Lamar Buffalo Ranch here and brought in 21 bison from two private herds to breed with the remaining wild bison in an effort to bring the species back from the brink. The irony that the Army, great restorer of bison to Yellowstone, had been the federal government's primary instrument in efforts to eradicate the species from the frontier as a means to control Indigenous peoples isn't lost on historians.

Regardless, the plan worked, and by 1954, some 1300 bison grazed in the abundant grassland of the Lamar Valley. With the bison coming back so strong, the Park Service periodically culled the growing herd, either by removing animals to start or supplement herds on other public and tribal lands, or by killing them, with the meat given to Indigenous peoples or relief agencies. In 1969, public outrage over the killing of the nation's most beloved ungulate resulted in a moratorium on culling the Yellowstone herd, and the bison population shot up accordingly, increasing sixfold (from 500 to 3000 animals) over the next two decades.

LAMAR BUFFALO RANCH

The Lamar Buffalo Ranch, located about 10 miles east of Tower Junction off Highway 212, still exists today, but the site isn't used for bison breeding any longer. Instead, the small campus of backwoods buildings and fenced enclosures is maintained as a historic district and also serves as the home of Yellowstone Forever, a nonprofit that works in tandem with the National Park Service to protect, preserve, and enhance Yellowstone through education and philanthropy. The group's enlightening field seminars led by conservation biologists, professional photographers, and other experts are open to the public and well worth the price of admission.

Meanwhile, the park's elk herds were also on the rise, leading to increased competition for forage. This perfect storm of rebounding wildlife led hordes from both species outside park borders in search of greener pastures. Unfortunately, private landowners and ranchers weren't too keen on these wild ungulates trampling their fences and raiding their livestocks' forage, let alone potentially transmitting brucellosis, a bacterial disease inducing abortions or still-births that these wild ungulates can pass on to domestic animals sharing rangeland. Beyond national park boundaries, elk and bison could be shot on sight, which allowed for some culling of both herds.

Nowadays a multi-agency roadmap called the Interagency Bison Management Plan (IBMP) guides the management of bison in Yellowstone. The stakeholders, including five government agencies and three tribal entities, work together to maintain a wild and free-ranging bison population while mitigating the risk of brucellosis transmission.

While IBMP has improved relations between ranchers and conservationists, biologists still think the park's bison population is too high, especially in the Lamar Valley. A 2020 study by researchers from Oregon State University found the abundance of hungry bison has stripped most of the valley's floral diversity, degrading the habitat available to other species more common here before.

One of those species is the American beaver, once plentiful across the Lamar Valley but now rarely encountered. Ungulate overabundance has forced hungry elk and bison to make do with twigs, leaves, and small branches from trees, denuding the valley of willow, aspen, and cottonwood. With these trees go the beavers, who use them as food and building materials for their dams and lodges. The Lamar Valley used to host dozens of active beaver colonies along its 20-mile course—these days one or two is the norm, and some years there are none.

In any case, the debate rages on over what to do about bison overgrazing here, with some advocating for more human intervention and others for extending the laissez-faire policy of natural regulation—that is, letting the ecosystem and its inhabitants sort it out on their own. Regardless, the bison's comeback from the brink of extinction is a success story that couldn't have happened without the existence of Yellowstone National Park as a sanctuary.

Cut to the present, and there's a new conservation success story playing out in the Lamar Valley: the return of the gray wolf. Indeed, this remote valley in the northeast corner of Yellowstone, once devoid of gray wolves, now has the greatest density of the animals per square mile of any place in the United States.

Before white settlement, as many as two million gray wolves roamed the continent from coast to coast. While these carnivorous canids posed little direct threat to humans, their predation on livestock threatened settlers' way of life. As such, most gray wolves met the wrong end of a rifle. By the late 1960s, they were gone everywhere in the Lower 48 except a small swath of the northern Midwest, where fewer than 1000 hung on.

After years of lobbying by conservationists, the federal government finally acceded to requests to protect gray wolves under the Endangered Species Act in 1978. Part of this designation requires that efforts be made to restore endangered species to their former native territory, and as such, the idea of reintroducing gray wolves to Yellowstone percolated among wildlife biologists, conservationists, and like-minded policymakers.

In 1987, the US Fish & Wildlife Service (FWS), the federal agency charged with administering the endangered species program, released its Northern Rocky Mountain Wolf Recovery Plan, including a proposal to introduce an experimental population of wolves into Yellowstone. In 1991, Congress finally funded an environmental impact statement on restoring wolves to the park; three years after that the Secretary of the Interior signed off on the reintroduction plan.

On January 12, 1995, eight gray wolves from western Canada were trucked into Yellowstone and put into acclimation pens for several weeks before eventually being released into the wilds of the Lamar Valley. Over the next two years,

‹ A wolf from the Druid Peak pack, which was relocated here from western Canada in 1996.

33 more gray wolves from Canada and northwestern Montana joined them.

The transplanted wolves made themselves right at home. By 2003, the initial experimental population of 41 wolves had reproduced and grown to 174 animals spread across sixteen different packs inhabiting Yellowstone.

And go figure, elk numbers began to decrease markedly. As many as 25,000 elk had roamed Yellowstone National Park in the early 1990s; today as few as 5000 remain, thanks in large part to the return of their natural predator. The reintroduced wolves preyed on older, weak, and injured elk, thereby creating smaller, stronger herds. Wary of their ancient predator, elk browsed less in open areas like streambeds, where trees like willow could regenerate; this sparked the return of beavers and a host of other wildlife. While park managers struggled for a century to keep elk numbers in check across Yellowstone in the absence of predators, it only took a few short years for a relatively small number of wolves to do the job on their own and restore a long-lost balance to the ecosystem.

These days, just shy of 100 gray wolves live year-round within Yellowstone's borders, down from the peak of 174 in the mid-2000s. What happened between then and now to precipitate such a decline? The short answer is drought. The worst drought in 1200 years grips the American West, likely correlated with the onset of climate change, reducing forage throughout the Lamar Valley and other regions near and far. Many elk that spent at least summer here have left the park for less crowded, greener pastures. Some of the wolves have followed; indeed, the vast majority of the reintroduced wolves' 500-plus strong diaspora now lives beyond park boundaries, spreading hundreds of miles across Greater Yellowstone and firmly reinstated as a keystone species whose health reflects that of its larger ecosystem.

After several court cases, Yellowstone's gray wolves were finally taken off the endangered species list in 2017, and as such, can now be hunted if they are outside of the national park on state land during regulated seasons. The program is managed and administered by FWS, which continues to monitor wolves around Yellowstone and has the option to relist the species if its recovery is not sustained. (A recent decision by FWS to relist an over-hunted Great Lakes

population of gray wolves has no bearing on Yellowstone's wolves, which remain delisted as of this writing.)

So far, FWS hasn't had to step in to protect Yellowstone's wolves, but that could change given the uptick in wolf kills in Idaho and Montana, as those states removed quota limits on wolf hunting in 2021. In the first year after the quotas were lifted, more than 500 wolves out of around 2600 were killed by hunters in Idaho and Montana. That kill rate could rise as more hunters participate. Only time will tell if these trends necessitate relisting Yellowstone's beleaguered wolves as threatened or endangered.

If you've come to the Lamar Valley to try to see some wolves for yourself, you won't be alone: Packs of wolf-crazed human visitors often convoy, with spotting scopes, binoculars, and telephoto lenses in tow. While six different packs of wolves have spread out across Yellowstone, the Junction Butte pack here in the Lamar Valley (now two dozen wolves strong) might be the most visible.

Of course, it wouldn't be America's Serengeti without a few more iconic wildlife species to complete the scene. Other mammals roaming these parts include grizzly and American black bears, cougars, coyotes, red foxes, badgers, mule deer, pronghorn, bighorn sheep, and red squirrels. Meanwhile, birders flock here to catch glimpses of more than 40 different avian species including trumpeter swan, harlequin duck, sandhill crane, golden eagle, peregrine falcon, red-naped sapsucker, pine siskin, willow flycatcher, savannah sparrow, brown-headed cowbird, and lazuli bunting, among others. For lovers of wildlife, the Lamar Valley is the jackpot.

Above, from left: A bison and its calf trek the Lamar Valley while a gaggle of Canada geese look on from the riverside.

A trumpeter swan begins to take flight.

Continuing on Highway 212, about 2.5 miles east of where the road veers off from the Lamar River, park at the small arked pullout on the southeast side of the road to check out Soda Butte, namesake of the river tributary here. One of the few reminders of Yellowstone's geothermal reputation in the otherwise calm Lamar Valley, this travertine mound formed more than a century ago when calcium carbonate precipitated from an underground hot spring. Over time, the travertine built up around the spring's vent to its current height of 20 feet.

A gold prospector who camped in the area named the butte after what he mistakenly thought was sodium carbonate (also known as "soda" ash) spewing out of it. Really it was calcium carbonate, but the name stuck. While Soda Butte hardly emits the water and gases it used to, passersby can still sometimes detect a faint sulfur smell nearby. Since the flaky travertine is very fragile, it's illegal to touch or climb on Soda Butte—and it's also not worth the risk of being burned by acidic hydrothermal water or steam.

When you've marveled enough at the strange sight, hit the valley's last stretch. Within another two road miles, the valley gives way to Douglas firs that suddenly crowd both sides of the highway. Look for the parking area and Trout Lake trailhead on the northwest side of the road. This short hike to a wild alpine lake (covered in another chapter of this book) gets you out of the car and far off the beaten path into true backcountry.

Whether or not you bother with the hike, the pullout here is as good a turnaround spot as any if you're heading back into the park. The benefits of making your way back the way you just came include a different perspective, lighting, and potential wildlife sightings.

If you aren't turning around, Highway 212 heads northeast, eventually leaving the park in Montana just west of the small community of Silver Gate on the western outskirts of Cooke City. Whether you go out and back or just one way through the Lamar Valley, you will certainly be glad you got to see America's Serengeti with your own eyes.

TROUT LAKE

Serene alpine lake with Absaroka mountain views and spawning trout

DIFFICULTY
Moderate

LOCATION
Northeast Yellowstone (Tower-Roosevelt)

HIKE LENGTH
2 miles

I f you love wildlife, forests, and alpine lakes, the hike to Trout Lake may be one of the shortest ways to check all three boxes—and put a big smile on your nature-loving face. Park at the small Lamar Valley pullout off Highway 212 about 10 road miles south of the park's Northeast Entrance Station. This small parking area can only fit about nine cars, but it's rarely more crowded than that. (Alternatively, you can park at another pullout nearby and walk along the road-side back to start the hike.)

Set out on foot from the well-marked trailhead. While the hike is relatively short, it does traverse some typically rough conditions, including mud, roots, and some elevation gain; hiking shoes or boots, or sturdy sneakers at a minimum, are recommended.

Initially, you'll make your way through an open meadow, with Wyoming big sagebrush dominating the landscape. Some lovely purple-pink Woods' roses brighten up the otherwise earthen and green scene. Look to the north to massive yet crumbling Mt. Hornaday, 10,003 feet in elevation, with columnar basalt flanks giving it a fortress-like appearance. If it's spring or early summer, scan the mountainside for cascading waterfalls as winter snowpack melts off. Although Mt. Hornaday looks tall from here, it's a shrimp compared to its peers in the Absaroka Range, where 123 different

A Woods' rose bloom brings welcome pink and yellow hues to the landscape. Later in summer, red squirrels, mule deer, coyotes, and bears munch on its rose hips, a good source of energy. ▾

From top: Trout Lake, surrounded by Douglas firs and sedges, sits in a small basin just shy of 7000 feet elevation in the Lamar Valley of northeast Yellowstone.

The columnar basalt flank of Mt. Hornaday emerges from a lush conifer forest.

named peaks top 11,500 feet. At 13,153 feet, Francs Peak tops them all.

The trail heads west and slightly uphill, and within another tenth of a mile, tucks into the woods. This forest is dominated by Rocky Mountain Douglas fir, with a healthy dose of quaking aspen and Engelmann spruce for good measure.

While this spot may be in the foothills of the towering Absaroka range, at less than 7000 feet it's still lower in elevation than much of Yellowstone. The Yellowstone plateau averages 8000 feet in elevation, perfect for lodgepole pines, which dominate 80 percent of the park's forests accordingly. In this slightly lower, wetter stretch of the park's northeast corner, other tree species have a better chance, and the resulting mixed forest here provides a welcome relief to the dark, dense lodgepole forests elsewhere around Yellowstone.

You'll notice the difference as soon as you enter the woods. A small stand of quaking aspen trees welcomes you into this open woodland with outstretched boughs supporting hundreds of glinting oval leaves reflecting light every which way. While several different aspens are at attention here, truth be told, the entire stand is a single organism, springing from the soil all at once and growing side-by-side in uniform, genetically programmed amounts. In fact, each aspen trunk is more appropriately called a clone than a tree.

Moving through the aspens, Douglas fir branches close in overhead. These big trees—some north of 200 feet tall, 6 feet in diameter, and 400 years old—dominate this stretch of woodland. This scene change provides for a much different feel under the canopy than lodgepole forests. Here, there

Canada geese make themselves
at home on the banks of Trout Lake.

‹ The complex, colorful design of a sticky geranium bloom is a big draw for bees and other insect pollinators.

is more space between trunks for understory shrubs and wildflowers. Arrowleaf balsamroot, silky lupine, and sticky geranium vie for scant openings, adding dashes of color to the forest floor.

You'll probably notice some of the Douglas firs here have black charring around their lower buttresses, proving they lived through at least one forest fire, probably more. Their thick, furrowed bark protects their inner cambium—the lifeblood that transports nutrients from roots to tips—from licking flames, allowing them to survive all but the most apocalyptic wildfires. (Contrast this against typically spindly, dense stands of thin-barked lodgepole pines, which tend to fall like matchsticks when raging burns pass through.)

These relatively rare Douglas fir forests provide sustenance for a range of wildlife. Yellow-rumped warbler, dark-eyed junco, mountain chickadee, and American robin are among the forest songbirds here that love the trees' nutritious seeds, plucking them directly from downward-hanging cones. Least chipmunks and red squirrels are also big fans, fattening themselves up on seeds late summer through fall, and caching what they can't eat for winter. Grizzly and black bears do their best Winnie-the-Pooh impressions by sucking the sweet sap out of crevices in the bark. (Given the preponderance of bears in this area, be prepared with bear spray and make a lot of noise while you hike to signal your presence.)

Engelmann spruce is another tree you'll encounter here, distinguished by its unique single green needles that are

◂ A Douglas fir tree clings to the shoreline of Trout Lake.

▴ Grasses and sedges line the trail that circles Trout Lake.

squared off on the edge and sharp to the touch. The tree's 1.5-inch-long cones are covered in papery scales. Wood from these trees is prized by luthiers (guitar makers) for its resonant, mid-range, tonally smooth sound when used in an acoustic guitar's top. Given their value, Engelmann spruce are increasingly rare in the wild; luckily, places like Yellowstone exist, where timber cutting for commercial purposes is forever banned.

The trail switches back and forth a couple of times, winding past some of the bigger trees in the park and most of the hike's 150-foot elevation gain. After a quarter mile in the woods, you'll reach its high point at a saddle in the shadow of a sprawling, ancient Douglas fir. Looking west through the trees, you'll get your first glimpse of Trout Lake's sparkling surface. A few more steps land you on its serene southeastern shoreline, elevation 6962 feet.

This perfect little 12-acre lake is rimmed on its far side in a sea of green grasses and sedges. You've made it this far, so you may as well follow the trail all the way around. Go right and follow the lake's tree-lined eastern shore. After about a tenth of a mile, the trees give way to a grassy tapestry.

Common beaked sedge and blister sedge, both obligate wetlands species—they only occur in wetlands—have taken over sections of this shoreline. Although these two herbaceous cousins are native to the region, they can sometimes crowd out other plants vying to survive. In opposition to this monocultural tendency, small-wing sedge, bluejoint reedgrass, alpine bluegrass, Idaho fescue, alpine timothy, and tufted hairgrass mix it up in the near-shore ecosystem. Meanwhile, parsnipflower buckwheat, western serviceberry, and cow parsnip make leafy green cameos in the riot of grass.

In yet another tenth of a mile, the trail crosses a wooden footbridge over Trout Lake's feeder creek, a tributary of larger Soda Butte Creek, which meanders to the northeast. If it's late spring or summer, look for Yellowstone cutthroat trout, native to this part of the Intermountain West, battling their way upstream en route to natal spawning grounds. These fish are an important food source for raptors, bears, mink, and river otters, but their numbers have dwindled in recent decades due to myriad factors. One of the biggies is competition from, predation by, and in some cases hybridization with non-native fish. Another is the hard-to-control spread of a microscopic non-native protozoan parasite that causes so-called whirling disease in infected trout, resulting in skeletal deformities that inhibit their ability to swim—and as such, make them easy pickings for predators. As if these hurdles weren't enough, climate change is making for inhospitable living conditions in the waterways these native fish have traditionally inhabited, with water levels too low and temperatures too high.

Yellowstone cutthroat trout make their way upstream in Trout Lake's feeder creek on the way to their natal spawning grounds. ▾

The good news is native fish in these upper reaches are doing better than down in Yellowstone Lake. And since the release of a multiagency conservation plan for Yellowstone's native fish in 2010, biologists have implemented a range of methods to selectively

* River otters love to fish around Trout Lake and frolic in its shoreline meadows.

remove non-native fish and improve habitat specifically for Yellowstone cutthroats.

While biologists familiar with the Yellowstone cutthroat's plight consider it sensitive from a conservation standpoint, the US Fish & Wildlife Service has thus far resisted listing the species as threatened under the US Endangered Species Act—perhaps because so much of its habitat remains on protected land, and fishermen already are supposed to release any they catch. That said, if you do cast a line in Trout Lake, you'll need a fishing permit from the National Park Service and to stay away from the inlet creek and cove, which are protected as spawning grounds. Make sure to release any smaller fish (14 to 20 inches long) with the signature red streak under the jawline, as these native Yellowstone cutthroats deserve to live another day and do their part to repopulate the region's waterways. Otherwise, anglers are free to keep, and eat, any non-native rainbow trout (they are 20 to 30 inches long and do not have a red line under their jaw)—and are actually helping the conservation cause by doing so.

Just because humans aren't allowed to fish the inlet creek and cove doesn't mean wildlife will stay away. Indeed, many a hiker to Trout Lake has been honored with sightings of river otters fishing the stream and cavorting on the verdant wetland banks. Though this rambunctiousness may look like old-fashioned play, it may serve multiple practical purposes, including strengthening social bonds, practicing hunting techniques, and scent-marking the landscape. Since these

* An osprey picks up a Yellowstone cutthroat trout lunch to go.

semi-aquatic, 4-foot-long, 20-pound mammals are so active, they need to eat a lot—and that's a big part of the reason they are so commonly seen around Trout Lake, where fishing is easy. You're more likely to see them early morning or late afternoon, as they spend most daylight hours holed up in underground dens near the shoreline.

Also don't be surprised if an enterprising osprey swoops down and nabs a tail-a-flapping trout. Both grizzly and black bears love catching fish here as well, so make a lot of noise and move slowly to give them time to know you're here, especially since they may be distracted by the good fishing. If you don't actually see bears, you will likely see a few big piles of their scat, which is always a good reminder to stay alert.

Follow the narrow foot trail along the inlet creek as long as you like, then turn around and continue circumnavigating the lakeshore. When you reach the opposite side, you'll cross over the lake's outlet stream, which tumbles downhill to the north. Wildflowers spill over the edges of this aquatic ribbon as views of Druid Peak open up to the west.

Keep circling the lake, and after another quarter mile along its west side, the trail rejoins the forest and delivers

⌃ Look for heroic rainbow and Yellowstone cutthroat trout making their way up the inlet creek that channels snowmelt from higher ground into Trout Lake.

you back to the junction where you began the lollipop loop. Turn right and head back down the way you came. With only two short hiking miles and practically a lifetime's worth of nature views under your belt, this experience is sure to rank highly against any short day hike in Yellowstone or beyond, so make sure to savor every minute.

ARTIST POINT TO LILY PAD LAKE

Canyon and waterfall views on the way to a picturesque, lily pad-covered lake

DIFFICULTY
Easy

LOCATION
Central Yellowstone (Canyon Village)

HIKE LENGTH
2 miles

The short, level hike starting from Artist Point offers not only great views of thunderous Lower Falls and the Grand Canyon of the Yellowstone but also transports you to a serene alpine lake where you might even find a little solitude amidst the hubbub of one of the park's busiest sections.

Park at the Artist Point parking lot if you can find a space. On a warm summer day, it's not unheard of for all 100 spots to fill; if so, just wait for a bit, as most visitors spend less than 20 minutes taking in the view before rolling on to their next stop. Once you've parked, pick up the well-marked South Rim Trail heading east and walk for less than a tenth of a mile to Artist Point proper, where the National Park Service maintains a lookout spot carved out of the stone at the top of the canyon rim.

◄ Lower Falls and the Grand Canyon of the Yellowstone framed by lodgepole pine trees.

Pink, orange, yellow, gray, off-white, green, and brown make up the canyon's unique color palette. ◄

Peering over the edge, look west, and follow the course of the mighty Yellowstone River to majestic Lower Falls, perfectly framed by flanking canyon walls. This 308-foot cascade (twice as tall as Niagara Falls) is the biggest, most famous waterfall in Yellowstone—and the second-most photographed site in the national park after Old Faithful. In spring, when snow is draining out of the mountains above, upwards of 60,000 gallons of water per second flow over Lower Falls. In fall and winter, the flow can dwindle to only 5000 gallons per second, sometimes in the form of icy showers.

The canyon walls are composed of a mixture of rhyolite, a pale, fine-grained volcanic granite containing distinct crystalline particles, and tuff, a light, porous rock formed by the consolidation of volcanic ash. Hydrothermal features, which reveal themselves at odd spots along the vertical canyon walls with mysterious puffs of steam, are primarily responsible for the orange, yellow, pink, gray, and off-white coloration of the canyon walls, tormented over the eons by untold hot water mineral baths and acid washes like so many other sections of Yellowstone National Park.

The canyon's origins can be traced to the massive eruption around 640,000 years ago that created the 1500-square-mile volcano we now know as the Yellowstone caldera. It wasn't until the 1970s, a century after the creation of the national park, that geologists began to realize Yellowstone was actually a huge, 30- by 45-mile caldera. Not to be confused with a crater (which is formed by the outward explosion of rocks and other material from a volcano), a caldera comes from an inward collapse after an eruption, followed by infilling from lava flows and sediments.

Eventually, perhaps 500,000 years after Yellowstone's initial eruption, this infill started to erode along an ancient fault line, and what we now know as the Grand Canyon of the Yellowstone began to emerge. Of course, the original version of the canyon wasn't as wide or long as what we see now. Erosion and glacial outburst floods walloped the weaker outer layers of rock, creating the huge chasm beloved today. In this violent scenario that played out across the Intermountain West at the end of the last ice age, ice dams that had built up started to melt out and give way, unleashing tsunami-like floodwaters that scraped out existing valleys into ever deeper chasms. Subsequent millennia

‹ You can often spot rainbows at or near the misty base of Lower Falls on a sunny day.

▲ Thomas Moran's 1872 painting "The Grand Canyon of the Yellowstone" is among the works of art that helped convince Congress to create Yellowstone National Park later that year.

of erosional weather forces shaped the variegated canyon walls into what we see today from Artist Point.

In all, the Grand Canyon of the Yellowstone stretches nearly 24 miles, dropping as much as 1200 vertical feet from rim to river, and chasming between .3 and .75 miles across.

And the view from Artist Point is sublime. Members of the Hayden Expedition agreed back when they surveyed the area in 1871 in order to advise the government on what to do with this spectacular region. In fact, Artist Point is likely one of several spots around the canyon where expedition member Thomas Moran made sketches for his epic painting "The Grand Canyon of the Yellowstone," which helped convince Congress to create Yellowstone National Park in 1872.

If it's a sunny day, look toward the base of the falls to see if you can spot a rainbow emanating from the mists below. Rainbows aren't just celestial phenomena; all it takes to form one is bright sunlight, water droplets suspended in the air, and the right point of perspective on the scene. You'll have these ingredients in abundance as you walk the South Rim Trail.

Now that you've seen Lower Falls, take a moment to hear it. Close your eyes and listen for the falls' rumble, which must be deafening at their base given how loud it is even here, almost a mile away and a quarter mile down.

▴ Bark detail, lodge-pole pine.

◂ A young lodgepole pine firmly rooted in the steeply graded canyon hillside.

When you've had your fill of the sights and sounds of Lower Falls—not to mention the throngs of other onlookers vying for the best selfie—head east on the South Rim Trail toward Lily Pad Lake. You'll get plenty of additional opportunities to stare into the mottled, multicolored canyon while making your way along the well-maintained trail, and the crowds thin just a few feet past the Artist Point viewing area.

Like elsewhere in Yellowstone, just about all the trees you'll see are lodgepole pines. Young ones pop out of rock crevices here and there, with little green needle balls that look like mini pompoms. Meanwhile, gnarled, older lodgepoles hover like helicopter parents, some growing at

45-degree angles from nearly vertical canyon walls, stalky branches elbowing out to collect even more sunlight. The contrast between parched, scarred canyon walls and verdant forest a few feet from the chasm's edge is remarkable.

In spring and summer, wildflowers dress up the trailsides. Silvery lupines are an understory fixture here. Each branched stem is lined with silvery-green leaves and grows from one to two feet tall, blooming in violet fused-petal winglets in late spring and early summer. You'll also notice heartleaf arnica, identified by its heart-shaped green leaves that form a carpet underneath showy yellow summer blooms. Another wildflower to keep an eye out for here is golden ragwort, a daisy family member that clusters at the edge of rocks or fallen logs and sports yellow eight-petaled blooms.

Meanwhile, the cute pointy leaves of grouse whortleberry lend a tinge of green to the shady understory. In late summer, this miniature member of the huckleberry family explodes with small, dark red berries beloved by birds, bears, and humans alike.

One native bird species rightfully associated with grouse whortleberry is the dusky grouse, largest of three species of mountain grouse in the Greater Yellowstone ecosystem. These chicken-sized dark blue birds are rarely seen but sometimes heard, especially if you happen to hike by one roosting under a shrub. If you hear a series of five soft, low-pitched hoots, it might be wise to back away, so as not to roust an already skittish dusky.

These grouse gorge themselves on whortleberries in fall to fatten up to overwinter in higher-altitude spots with deeper snowbanks, where they burrow in for the season. Duskies only surface occasionally in winter to forage for conifer tips, their only sustenance until the spring buffet of beetles and plants reopens.

Below, from top: Golden ragwort brightens up patches of the forest floor with its summertime yellow blooms.

Grouse whortleberry, a huckleberry family member.

No one knows for sure why these alpine fowl head for higher, colder, snowier sites rather than migrate to lower ground like most animals. One reason might be to avoid competitors for needles—another might be to avoid predators. Dusky grouse make an easy meal for local carnivorous mammals and raptors of all stripes.

Speaking of raptors, look for ospreys flying around on air currents over the canyon in search of prey. Dozens of these black and white "fish hawks" migrate here in late spring to mate, and they nest atop eroded pinnacles throughout the canyon. Soon after, females lay clutches of two to four eggs, which take six to eight weeks to incubate. Within a few short months, the downy-feathered juveniles reach nearly full size and start to look like their parents, at which point the family abandons its nest, scattering to the four winds and the best perches near favorite fishing spots.

Of course, ospreys aren't the only birds using canyon walls as habitat. Golden and bald eagles are frequently sighted here, soaring above the canyon or perching on outcrops in search of an easy meal. Meanwhile, cliff swallows nestle in overhangs, where they can take cover but still easily access the flying insects they prefer to eat.

Another bird that often lives on the cliff walls is the common raven. These black corvids (closely related to crows) are considered some of the smartest, most adaptable birds. They range far and wide to dine on a variety of prey including beetles, fish, small rodents, baby birds, and even

• Lily Pad Lake is a serene gem not far from the throngs of Artist Point.

Opposite, from top: Dusky grouse love to munch on grouse whortleberries in fall before they head uphill to overwinter.

Dusky grouse subsist primarily on needle tips of lodgepole pines in winter.

An osprey pair guards their nest.

carrion scavenged from other predators' kills. These enterprising birds have even been known to alert wolves to the presence of carrion so they can feast on scraps left behind.

Just shy of a half mile on the trail, look for a sign pointing you to the right, toward Lily Pad Lake. Heading south, you'll tuck into the woods as dense stands of lodgepole pine crowd both sides of the trail, and you'll no longer have canyon views to distract you.

Another third of a mile, and you'll see the pretty lake glistening through the lodgepoles. As you approach, you'll notice how this little lake got its name: Sections are practically covered in Indian pond lilies. This aquatic herbaceous plant, common in lakes, ponds, and quiet streambanks across the Yellowstone caldera, develops shiny, leathery green leaves and blooms into lovely yellow lotus-shaped flowers in late spring and early summer. It is a favorite forage of beaver and muskrat but is also considered a delicacy by beetles, porcupines, deer, and moose, among others.

Aerenchyma, a spongy tissue in the lily's leaves, transports oxygen from the air above the water's surface down into the plant's rhizomatous roots while exhaling methane gas otherwise trapped in sediment on the lake bottom. This exchange of gasses helps lilies and other aquatic plants maintain a balance of nutrients. Indian pond lilies are

thriving in Yellowstone; outside the park, they're threatened by human development, while lilies everywhere are at risk from climate change.

Yellowstone's pond lilies are precious for the wildlife they attract. A patient naturalist observing these lilies might spot a boreal chorus frog or spotted frog, or even a boreal toad or blotched tiger salamander—all four amphibians are native to the Greater Yellowstone ecosystem. You might also spot a wandering garter snake, valley garter snake, or rubber boa slithering along the shoreline; these three reptiles are also native to Yellowstone's wetland habitats.

‹ The Grand Canyon of the Yellowstone formed around 130,000 years ago, when infill from the huge eruption that formed the Yellowstone caldera eroded along an ancient fault line.

‹ Indian pond lilies provide habitat for a range of insects and amphibians, as well as forage for beaver, muskrat, moose, and deer—but also serve as a natural venting system.

Enjoy this serene lakeside setting as long as you wish, then retrace your steps back to Artist Point. You'll get a new, opposite perspective of the canyon on the last stretch of the return hike—not to mention the sun will be at a different angle in the sky, casting the canyon walls in different colors.

Back at Artist Point and the parking lot, you'll be glad you made the extra effort to get off the beaten path a bit at Lily Pad Lake. And you won't soon forget the view, one of America's most sublime, of thunderous Lower Falls and the majestic Grand Canyon of the Yellowstone.

HAYDEN VALLEY

Two-lane road through the heart of Yellowstone wildlife habitat "where the buffalo roam"

LOCATION
East-Central Yellowstone (between Canyon Village and Lake Village)

DIFFICULTY
Easy

DRIVE LENGTH
16 miles

The 16-mile drive between Canyon Village and Fishing Bridge through Hayden Valley is one of the most popular places in the park to see wildlife, but that shouldn't scare you away. Indeed, as long as there are American bison at Yellowstone, you're almost guaranteed to see large numbers here. This verdant valley is also primary habitat for a range of other species, including grizzly and American black bear, gray wolf, Rocky Mountain elk, river otter, trumpeter swan, and many others.

Given that early mornings and late afternoons are the best times to see wildlife in Hayden Valley, time your drive accordingly. Getting out early or late in summer also lessens the chances of crowds—and potentially long traffic backups. From Canyon Junction, drive south on the Grand Loop Road through stands of lodgepole pine for about 4.5 miles until you reach a pullout on the north side of the road at Alum Creek that can fit about 15 cars. This will be your first sighting of the Hayden Valley as it spreads out to the east and south, so stop and have a look around. This pullout is directly above a big curve in the Yellowstone River, and you'll often see Canada geese browsing on riparian grasses and American white pelicans fishing in the river.

These are far from the only birds you'll encounter traversing the Hayden Valley—indeed, birders may feel like they've died and gone to heaven here. Keep your eyes peeled for northern harriers flying low sorties above the Yellowstone River marshes, in search of a quick meal of deer mouse or lesser scaup. Yellow-rumped warblers flit about willowy areas near the water's edge. Trumpeter swans cruise the slow-moving curves in the river, nibbling aquatic plants as they go. Golden eagles are surprisingly bold in their hunting, sometimes opting for prey as big and feisty as red foxes—although picking off a Yellowstone cutthroat trout from the water's surface is more typical of this adaptable predator.

‹ The Yellowstone River meanders through the verdant Hayden Valley.

Take your time gawking at the splendid view and any wildlife drama that might be unfolding. When you're ready, head south for another mile to the Hayden Valley Overlook, smack dab in the middle of this verdant valley. One of the iconic views of the national park here warrants getting out of the car for a closer look than can be afforded through the windshield.

In the foreground, silver sagebrush is the dominant plant on the relatively parched upland plateau of the overlook, with plenty of Junegrass, Columbia needlegrass, Richardson needlegrass, slender wheatgrass, and thickspike wheatgrass as well. Woolly locoweed and silky lupine burst forth in showy blue and violet blooms, while spreading phlox offsets the beige surroundings with its cute clusters of five-petaled white flowers. Far more vegetation spreads out in the moist grasslands below, where the Yellowstone River naturally irrigates the riparian wetlands of this wide, U-shaped glacial valley.

Like the other major valleys of the Yellowstone caldera, Hayden Valley was formed as a result of two different ice ages and the melting of the piedmont glaciers here as temperatures warmed. The glacial till and outwash left behind when the glaciers retreated became fertile ground for a

American bison bulls can weigh 2000 pounds, making them the largest of all North American mammals. ▾

dozen or so native grasses and sedges, which compete for real estate here at the valley bottom. Water sedge, slender tufted-sedge, Columbian sedge, broadscale sedge, Raynolds' sedge, shortbeak sedge, wire rush, tufted hairgrass, Kentucky bluegrass, Idaho fescue, meadow barley, and mountain brome are among the perennials making Hayden Valley a lush oasis of life.

Perhaps nobody loves the grassy vegetation of this grand ecosystem more than the American bison. Hayden Valley is one of the best places to see these burly ungulates that once covered the Great Plains as far as the eye could see. Yellowstone is now the only place left where they have lived continuously since prehistoric times.

Bison graze 9 to 11 hours a day on fresh grass and sedge shoots, which deliver more protein pound for pound than the alfalfa farmers feed their livestock. The ability to dig through snowbanks by swinging their large heads back and forth allows them to forage even in the long Yellowstone winter. Like other ruminants (cattle, deer, moose, elk, sheep, goats), bison have multi-chambered stomachs and regurgitate their food for re-chewing, which helps make it possible for them to digest as much as 45 pounds of roughage a day. Unlike other ruminants, they process food more efficiently (and thus forage on lower-quality browse) thanks to especially large digestive tracts, giving them access to nutrition sources others decline.

But who eats bison? Only grizzly bears and gray wolves can take down an adult bison, but plenty of scavengers—coyotes, golden eagles, and ravens, to name a few—join in after the kill. Of course, dozens of bison die every year in accidents (like falling into hot springs), as well as from freezing or starving to death over winter; these carcasses help keep the scavengers fed.

In summer, the bison rut is on. Courting males grunt and stir up dirt in attempted displays of dominance, occasionally butting heads, locking horns, and trying to move one another away from a given female. Once a successful match is made, a bison's gestation period is nine months. Rusty red calves are born in spring, each weighing 30 to 70 pounds at birth. These big babies nurse with mom for a year before fending for themselves.

Today, some 5000 of these cloven-hoofed ruminants roam throughout and sometimes beyond the borders of Yellowstone National Park, up from just 23 left in the region in the early 1900s, after they were slaughtered to the brink of extinction. In fact, the bison's recovery here has been so successful—they have a high survival rate, especially when free of the threat of human hunting, and their population here grows 10 to 17 percent annually—that park biologists

From top: Bison calves take about a year to wean themselves off their mothers' milk.

This grazing bison's longer winter coat is still falling off in a process called molting.

are forced to cull the herd by about 900 individuals every year to keep their population at a level the environment can support without being overloaded. Also, if the herd gets too large, groups of bison will head out of the park across invisible boundary lines in search of greener pastures, where they can be shot by local ranchers and hunters.

The Yellowstone herd is the largest on public land in the United States to this day and probably the only herd exhibiting wild behavior like their ancestors, in that they congregate in vast numbers during breeding season, as well as migrate to and explore new areas. The fact the Yellowstone herd has lots of habitat at its disposal and no culling by hunters inside park boundaries has allowed it to rebound to what park biologists consider a sustainable level.

The majority of bison in the herd stay around central Yellowstone for three seasons and head for lower altitudes around the park's western boundary or up in the Northern Range during winter. That said, some of the herd, typically the biggest, strongest males, stick it out here year-round.

While the herd is no longer threatened by hunting (as long as they stay within the park), other hazards challenge these horned beasts of the valley. One is brucellosis, a bacterial infection common in ruminants that can lead to miscarriages and reduced birth rates. Bison can be exposed to the bacteria that causes the disease when they come into contact with infected birth tissue from other ruminants utilizing the same range. (Bison, elk, and cattle tend to share low-elevation grasslands in late winter along river valleys outside park boundaries.) Brucellosis affects 10 to 15 percent of Yellowstone's bison population, which makes an impact but isn't catastrophic for the population's stability. That said, researchers believe bison can develop immunity to the infection after first exposure.

Regardless, make sure to stay out of danger near bison. These huge animals typically appear gentle, but they will charge if they feel threatened or encroached upon—and they can run 35 miles an hour (four times faster than you and I). Staying at least 25 yards away is a good rule of thumb. If you see the animal's tail stand up, back away (and get in your car if possible), as a charge could be imminent. While there's a lot of talk about bear maulings in Yellowstone, getting too close to a bison is just as potentially fatal—in fact, bison injure more park visitors than any other animal, year after year—so keep your distance and give them plenty of room to pass if they are so inclined.

The drive through Hayden Valley is only about a dozen miles, but it can be slow going given the risk of periodic bison jams—bison walking on or across the road, stopping traffic. If you're stuck in one, remember you're on vacation, not late for some appointment back at home, and you're probably going to get a close-up view of one or several bison as they weave around cars lined up to let them pass. And count your lucky stars, because it's much better to see a bison up close from safely inside your vehicle than outside it.

The view might not get any better than from the Hayden Valley Overlook, but continue south for fresh perspectives on this iconic landscape and the chance to see more wildlife. In two miles, pull over on the east side of the road at the Yellowstone River Overlook. Rocky Mountain elk often pass through in small groups. Great gray owls patrol the meadows for rodents and hares. Canada geese and cinnamon teals are among the waterfowl dabbling for aquatic insects and underwater vegetation in the river. American white pelicans and trumpeter swans may be floating on the river below in search of a quick meal. Bald eagles and ospreys divebomb the river, fast and furious, unbeknownst to the trout destined to be their next meal.

American white pelicans and Canada geese enjoy quiet stretches of the Yellowstone River as it meanders through the Hayden Valley. ▾

If you have a spotting scope, binoculars, or a camera with a telephoto lens, scan the forested hillside about two thirds of a mile to the east, especially where the grasslands give way to the trees. If you're lucky, you might catch sight of a bear out foraging—or even a mama bear trailing a few cubs and training them in the ways of the world. Yellowstone is home to two different species, black bears and grizzlies. Black bears, the smaller, less aggressive, and more likely to run away, are common across the United States. It's hard to get a read on the black bear population, as they are elusive and tend to stay far away from humans where they can. Biologists estimate some 400,000-plus roam the Lower 48 (only Delaware, Illinois, Indiana, Iowa, and Kansas have none), with another 100,000 or so in Alaska.

Here in Yellowstone, a robust population of 500 to 600 black bears lives large feeding on grasses, fruits, pine nuts, tree cambium, eggs, insects, trout, and the occasional elk calf, not to mention helping themselves to carrion left over from other predators' kills. Their claws are short and curved, perfect for climbing trees but not so good for digging up roots or ants like grizzlies'.

Black bears typically live 15 to 30 years and forage over a home range as big as 124 square miles. Boars (males) weigh between 210 and 315 pounds, while the daintier sows (females) tip the scales anywhere from 135 to 200 pounds. They mate in spring, and sows give birth the following winter while hibernating to a litter of between one and three cubs, who wait out the remaining winter months inside the den, fattening up on mother's milk. They debut in spring (usually late April), emerging into the light of day for the first time in their young lives.

Most visitors to Yellowstone between 1910 and 1970 had no problem seeing black bears, as the big beasts subsisted on food begged from humans traveling park roads. This was not good for the bears, who acclimated to human food and lost some of the ability and will to forage for themselves in nature, or for people, who put themselves in harm's way getting too close, in misguided efforts to feed bears or get photos. The frequent close contact between people and roadside black bears led to some 45 visitor injuries a year on average in the 1960s, with around 33 bears a year killed or removed from the park accordingly.

When the National Park Service finally banned visitors from feeding bears and set up bear-proof garbage containers around Yellowstone in 1970, the situation improved for everyone. These days, it's not uncommon for a year or more to go by without a single visitor injury from a black bear, with only one black bear killed or removed from the park every three years for transgressions against humans. Meanwhile, property damage from Yellowstone bears today is rare, down some 90 percent from the 1960s, when 219 bear-related claims was the annual average.

Nowadays, chances are good that if you spend enough time roaming Yellowstone, you will see a black bear, albeit hopefully nowhere near as close as the visitors of yore. Here in the Hayden Valley, train your eyes on the transition zones between the valley-bottom meadows and upland lodgepole pine forests. Black bears spend most of their time in the woods but occasionally make their way into the open, so don't forget to occasionally scan these edge zones for movement.

While far less common in Yellowstone than black bears, grizzly bears nevertheless take up a lot of bandwidth when it comes to visitor worries. And for good reason: grizzlies are Yellowstone's equivalent of the king of the jungle, an apex predator occupying the top of the food chain, who fears no others and takes what they want when they want it.

Grizzlies are a lot bigger than black bears. Males can weigh as much as 700 pounds and stand some three and a half feet tall at the shoulder. Besides their size, another way to distinguish a grizzly is its prominent shoulder hump from well-developed muscles it needs to dig for insects, grubs, and even burrowing rodents.

Grizzlies also need a lot more room to roam than their cousins. Indeed, a grizzly's home range can be as big as 2000 square miles, 16 times larger than a black bear's range. These agile predators can run 40 miles per hour (including up and down hills), climb trees, dig deep into the soil, and swim with ease, meaning that anything—from horse ants to Uinta ground squirrels to Rocky Mountain elk calves to Yellowstone cutthroat trout—can become a grizzly's next snack.

Only about 150 grizzly bears make their homes year-round in Yellowstone National Park proper, but more than 500 others are dispersed across the 34,000-square-mile Greater Yellowstone region, an area ten times larger than the park itself. While grizzlies were extirpated from most of the rest of the American frontier during the 19th century, a small population hung on in wild and remote Yellowstone.

Prior to white settlement, some 50,000 grizzlies roamed across the American West, living large in a world overflowing with a range of nutrients at their paw-tips. As the frontier was settled, hunting, trapping, and habitat loss conspired to decimate the grizzly bear's population across most of its historical range. By 1975, only about 1000 grizzlies were left in the Lower 48, and the federal government listed the species as threatened there under the Endangered Species Act. At the time, the US Fish & Wildlife Service, the federal agency in charge of the endangered species program, identified Greater Yellowstone as one of six recovery zones that could provide suitable habitat and room to roam for more grizzlies. (The other griz-friendly recovery zones are the Northern Continental Divide in and around Glacier National Park, the Cabinet-Yaaks in northwest Montana, Idaho's Selkirks, the Bitterroots along the Idaho-Montana border, and the North Cascades in Washington.)

While grizzlies haven't rebounded so well in those other zones, they have recovered nicely in Yellowstone in the intervening four-plus decades. Back in 1975, biologists estimated that 136 grizzlies occupied the Greater Yellowstone ecosystem; these days the number is closer to 730, with 150 of those calling the national park itself home. Over the years, these bears have managed to expand their occupied habitat by more than 50 percent. The fact that the number of grizzly sows producing cubs in the park has remained relatively stable for the last quarter century suggests that Yellowstone may be at or near its ecological carrying capacity (that is, the number of organisms an ecosystem can sustainably support) for grizzlies.

Indeed, the bears' very success could get them kicked off the threatened species list, which would mean they could be hunted when outside of national park boundaries. But so far none of the litigation to delist Yellowstone's grizzlies has borne fruit, and as such, the bears continue to enjoy the full protections their threatened status affords them. Whether or not you get to see a grizzly on your visit to the Hayden Valley or elsewhere in Yellowstone, isn't it enough to just know that they are still out there?

Of course, Hayden Valley is home to much more than just bears. Another mammal that spends time here grazing on sedges and grasses is the Rocky Mountain elk, and this hasn't gone unnoticed by Yellowstone's reintroduced and now recovered population of gray wolves. In fact, the twenty or so wolves in the Wapiti Lake Pack have denned on the west side of the Yellowstone River at the north end of Hayden Valley since 2016, occasionally trotting out into the

grasslands in search of a meal. A lone wolf can take down an elk calf all by itself, but nabbing a full-grown elk is a team effort, whereby several wolves chase and harass prey into exhaustion and submission. While the Wapiti Lake Pack has thrived here, the majority of Yellowstone's wolves are concentrated to the north, around the Lamar Valley.

⏴ Dusk is a great time to visit the Hayden Valley, both for the low-angled golden light and the chance to see wildlife at its most active.

If you're heading on to points south, Yellowstone River Overlook is your last chance to get out of the car and look around, so make the most of it. Like any of the pullouts along the Hayden Valley, this one makes for a lovely sunset viewing spot. And the fact that wildlife is more active at the edge of the day makes a sunset visit here that much more appropriate.

When you've inventoried the view from the overlook to your heart's content, say goodbye to the Hayden Valley for now. Heading south from here, the road re-enters the lodgepole forest in about three quarters of a mile, passing by the Field Mudpots to the west and the North Caldron and Forest Mudpot to the east. Just south of these thermal features is Mud Volcano, which is worth a stop (and a chapter). Regardless of where you head next, thoughts of Hayden Valley are sure to remain front and center whenever you think of Yellowstone.

MUD VOLCANO

DIFFICULTY
Easy

Still-spouting ancient thermal mudpots hint at a violent volcanic past

HIKE LENGTH
.75 mile

LOCATION
East-Central Yellowstone (between Canyon Village and Lake Village)

Mud Volcano marks the spot of one of the most unique, geothermally active regions of Yellowstone, delighting visitors with popping mud pots while also disgusting them with rotten-egg sulfur smells.

Three general types of geothermal features are present in Yellowstone. Alkaline-chloride geysers and springs, like Old Faithful and the Grand Prismatic Spring, developed in rhyolite underlays and have a slightly base pH (meaning, relatively, they are not very acidic). These types of features slowly precipitate sinter cones and sometimes produce colorful pools when thermophilic microbes settle in. Another type of thermal feature occurs in parts of the park underlaid with limestone—like Mammoth Hot Springs and New Terrace Drive—which is dissolved by hot underground water and results in travertine bubbling up to the surface and creating chalky white terraced hillsides.

Mud Geyser used to erupt muddy water as much as 50 feet in the air, but these days has settled down into a big, sizzling mudpot. ▾

Here at Mud Volcano, the third type of feature prevails, whereby low-pH (highly acidic) acid-sulfate fluids break down the very rock that hosts them. Sulfur and other corrosive vapors permeate the steam-rich thermal fluids here, which leads to the erosion of the volcanic rock pockets where pools form.

Clockwise from top: The green-tinged water of Mud Caldron is surrounded by yellow monkeyflower, Tweedy's rush, and swordleaf rush. Dragon's Mouth Spring lets off some steam in the distance.

Lodgepole pines proliferate on the outskirts of Mud Volcano.

Sizzling Basin.

While brown, bubbly pools may not be as scenic as other geothermal features around the park, they may be the hardest working if the constant churning and off-gassing here is any indication. During this process, called hydrothermal alteration, condensed steam mixes with air and local surface waters, which creates carbonic acid and sulfuric acid. The resulting acidic, magma-heated water can rapidly break down surrounding rocks and surface sediments into clay minerals, resulting in a muddy, bubbling, and sometimes colorful slurry in every depression in the landscape nearby. There's no better place to see this kind of feature in action than here at Mud Volcano.

Pick up the paved trail at the south end of the parking lot to do the loop in a counterclockwise direction (although any direction is fine). First, you'll pass Mud Caldron, a large green-tinged pool edged in milky, muddy foam that provides an apt introduction to the types of features you can expect on this loop.

Continue uphill on the paved path, which transitions to a boardwalk within another tenth of a mile and soon thereafter encounters Sizzling Basin, where a shallow, light gray pool bubbles like soda. In another 300 feet, you'll pass Churning Caldron, a formerly unheated pool until a series of earthquakes in 1978 and 1979 increased its temperature—nowadays, it's known to toss hot, muddy water three to five feet in the air.

Go left at a fork in the boardwalk to get a good look at Black Dragon's Caldron, a large, sizzling pond of mud that didn't exist until a fateful day in 1948, when a violent explosion turned what had been a quiet crack in the ground into a gurgling, sometimes eruptive visitor attraction. For several decades after coming to life, it erupted in explosive bursts, sending mud as much as 20 feet high. In recent decades, the caldron quieted and shifted a couple hundred feet to the southeast. It's anybody's guess if and when Black Dragon's Caldron will return to its previously explosive glory—or go back to sleep for decades.

A healthy stand of lodgepole pines to your immediate right knows which patches of earth here are hospitable to tree growth and which are just plain too acidic. In early summer, fireweed's magenta wands wave in the wind as they reach up from fallen log jumbles and other clearings. Double back to the previous junction, and continue as the boardwalk curves north through a patch where several fallen lodgepoles lay dead like so many dropped matchsticks, the result of the earthquakes that ripped through this active seismic zone five decades ago.

Soon you'll reach Grizzly Fumarole, a grouping of steaming holes in the ground that vary depending on the season. In dry summer months, they spew steam from mostly dry vents, while in fall and winter, they absorb rainfall and snowmelt and become mudpots.

Tweedy's rush and swordleaf rush populate some thermally compromised soils here. These green, pointy perennials thrive in soils where others don't dare. Likewise, yellow monkeyflower revels in poor-quality substrate. Its tubular, yellow-spotted corollas attract bees, butterflies, and hummingbirds. Prior to white settlement, Indigenous people commonly harvested the antioxidant-rich plant to eat raw, despite its bitterness.

From top: Grizzly Fumarole in its summer phase.

Mud Volcano used to throw mud dozens of feet in the air but eventually blew itself up, leaving an occasionally bubbling crater pool.

Drama at Dragon's Mouth Spring. ▸

The next feature along this *tour de mud* is the hike's namesake, Mud Volcano. While these days it's more a hole in the ground with a little bubbling water, it was quite the source of natural fireworks in the past. An interpretive sign details how explorers who stumbled onto Mud Volcano in 1870 watched in awe as it spewed mud into the surrounding treetops and shook the ground with each eruption. By the time Yellowstone was established in 1872, Mud Volcano had become just a pool of bubbling, muddy water like it is today—in the two intervening years, it had blown itself apart.

Don't skip the last feature here, Dragon's Mouth Spring, with a viewpoint 300 more feet north. It's a unique combination of geology and seismology featuring a small, dark cave backing up a pool of geothermally heated water, accompanied by noisy belches of steam at sporadic intervals—just like a dragon's mouth.

After that, retrace your steps toward the parking lot. Across the street and a bit north is Sulphur Caldron, an offset of the Mud Volcano group and the most acidic of all the geothermal features in Yellowstone; cross to check it out if you dare—its rotten egg odor is something fierce.

Seismology fans will also delight in (or be frightened by) the fact that Sour Creek Dome, the hill behind Sulphur Caldron to the east, is a resurgent dome of the Yellowstone supervolcano. This means the land moves up and down here with the fluctuation of the magma chamber roughly five miles below the surface. Scientists monitor domes like this one closely to gain insight into ongoing volcanic activity and to help detect oncoming earthquakes and volcanic eruptions.

No doubt you'll be glad to get the heck out of here, now that you know this! Back in the relative safety of your vehicle, you'll appreciate not only the colorful walk here, but that you've gained a new understanding of different kinds of geothermal features, and how each one alters the landscape around it in different but easily identifiable ways.

PELICAN CREEK NATURE TRAIL

Quintessential lodgepole forest trail to Yellowstone Lake shoreline

DIFFICULTY
Easy

HIKE LENGTH
.75 mile

LOCATION
East-Central Yellowstone (Fishing Bridge)

T his short hike crosses a variety of ecosystems, including lodgepole pine forest, sagebrush-covered dunes, and the wild and windy shoreline of Yellowstone Lake. Chances of spotting avian and other wildlife are good here, given these varied habitats.

Park at the turnout along the south side of Highway 14 (East Entrance Road) at the west end of Pelican Creek Bridge, just over a mile east of Fishing Bridge, where the Yellowstone River pours into Yellowstone Lake. The parking area can accommodate about 20 cars and is rarely full.

Pick up the well-marked trail heading southwest as it crosses over marshy ground bordering Pelican Creek and bisects a stand of mature lodgepoles. This stretch of woods, tucked in as it is between creek and lake, has been spared by wildfire, unlike nearby sections of the park. One result of this is these lodgepoles tend to be a little more spaced out compared to younger, newly regenerating stands, which are more dense and less inviting.

Given the trees' extra breathing room, more sunlight hits the forest floor, giving understory plants a bit

The variegated bark of lodgepole pine trees is your constant companion on this hike. ▾

▲ The Pelican Creek Nature Trail bisects a lodgepole forest besieged by deadfall trees, thanks to violent windstorms from nearby Yellowstone Lake.

Wolf lichens are ubiquitous on tree trunks and deadfalls throughout this lakeside forest. ▸

more of a boost. That said, you'll want to stay on the trail where maintenance crews have cleared the way, because deadfalls everywhere else make for treacherous walking otherwise. Howling winds from the big, flat expanse of Yellowstone Lake pummel this relatively exposed headland.

Many of the tree trunks here (living and dead) are covered by skeletal-looking yellow-green wolf lichens, which anchor to tree bark and grow slightly erect, gleaning nutrients and moisture from passing air currents.

Lichens are, in fact, a complex life form consisting of two different organisms—a fungus and an alga—that work together symbiotically to survive. The dominant partner is the fungus, which protects the underlying alga from the elements so it can photosynthesize and produce the energy both parties need to survive. The success of this symbiosis makes lichens one of the most widespread, adaptable types of organisms on the planet.

Besides dressing up the substrates they grow on, lichens provide valuable environmental services. One example is their ability to improve local air quality by filtering and absorbing airborne pollutants; indeed, scientists can monitor atmospheric levels of all kinds of contaminants in a given region by analyzing lichens, which retain traces of everything that pass their way. These little wonders of nature also play a role in tempering climate change by removing

Above, from left: Spreading phlox pretties up the ground in select spots near the lakeshore.

Silverleaf scorpion-weed is a favorite pollen source for bees.

atmospheric carbon dioxide and using it in photosynthesis to produce energy and generate oxygen.

After about a tenth of a mile, go right (west) at the fork to start the lollipop section of the loop. Make some noise as you hike and stay alert for grizzly bears, which frequent this area in spring and early summer, given the easy access to abundant fishing at both Pelican Creek and Yellowstone Lake.

After another tenth of a mile, head for a duney clearing up ahead dominated by low-slung mountain big sagebrush, but rife with other herbaceous plants and shrubs. Silky lupine lends chalky purple-blue to the scene, nicely offset by white flowers of spreading phlox. Slender cinquefoil sends up cute yellow five-lobed blooms. Silverleaf scorpionweed, woods strawberry, and common yarrow also make appearances, while orchard grass fills whatever gaps are left. This sweet, colorful meadow is a nice place to linger for a few minutes, but the lakeshore beckons.

Cross through one more neat row of lodgepoles and step out onto the rock-strewn but otherwise sandy beach fronting windswept Yellowstone Lake. Across the great expanse of the 139-square-mile lake, you'll see Elephant Back Mountain and Stephenson Island to the west; Frank Island and then Mount Sheridan and Flat Mountain to the south; and the towering Absaroka range to the east.

In the foreground, sandbars offshore host avian wildlife that make a living on the lake—Canada geese, avocets, black-necked stilts, great blue herons, double-crested cormorants, and of course American white pelicans. The latter bird, the nearby creek's namesake, frequents this watershed during spring and summer for the same reason as bears: to feast on Yellowstone cutthroat trout.

White pelicans need to eat about a quarter of their approximately 14-pound body weight every day for optimal nutrition, and they have been nesting here in Yellowstone Lake since time immemorial. (They fly south to the California and Gulf of Mexico coastlines in winter.)

Pelicans are among the 13 percent of bird species that nest in colonies. By definition, colonial nesters require a nest site surrounded by nests of other, similar birds in what's known as a rookery. Yellowstone's white pelicans nest primarily in the Molly Islands in the southeast arm of Yellowstone Lake. These two small islands are a quarter mile from the closest shore, and the National Park Service prohibits motorized boats from getting anywhere near them, to give the nesting birds space. Even though there is

▲ Yellowstone Lake is a wild place; keep an eye out for elk, bison, and bears wandering the shoreline.

American white pelicans, with the longest bills of any bird on the planet and 9-foot wingspans, are efficient predators of Yellowstone cutthroat trout. ▸

White pelicans patrol the shallows for fish where Pelican Creek meets Yellowstone Lake. ▸

only about an acre of land cumulatively between the Molly Islands, some 600-plus white pelicans nest there every year, not to mention dozens of double-crested cormorants and California gulls.

While that might seem like a lot of birds, biologists are worried about a mysterious, sharp decline in pelican numbers here over just the last two decades as of this writing. One theory holds that climate change has led to quicker spring melt-offs, temporarily but suddenly raising water levels in Yellowstone Lake, flooding the Molly Islands, and displacing birds from their nests at crucial junctures of the breeding season.

Another potential cause is the crash of Yellowstone cutthroat trout, the birds' primary food source here. While native cutthroats were already facing increasing environmental pressures (habitat loss, overfishing, climate change warming up their natal streams), the introduction of larger, non-native lake trout into Yellowstone Lake in the 1990s almost pushed them over the brink. The 20- to 30-inch lake trout can literally eat the 14- to 20-inch Yellowstone cutthroats for lunch—and they often do.

Of course, pelicans would be just as happy dining on lake trout as cutthroats. But the former's habit of swimming in deep water closer to the lake bottom means that the skimming pelicans can't get at them as easily as cutthroats, which tend to swim near the surface.

Park Service biologists have done heroic work to remove lake trout and have enlisted the help of the permitted angling public. But lake trout still dominate here, and only time will tell if efforts to dethrone this invader will bear fruit. Increasingly hungry pelicans must be keeping their webbed fingers crossed.

You could spend all day on the lakeshore staring at the birds and peaks, feeling contentedly small in the scheme of things. Whenever it is time to move it along, continue on the lollipop back into the lodgepoles, eventually to the junction where you'll retrace your steps. Pelican Creek is one walk you won't regret.

STORM POINT

Short, diverse hike to a windswept dunescape along Yellowstone Lake

DIFFICULTY
Easy

HIKE LENGTH
2.3 miles

LOCATION
East-Central Yellowstone (Fishing Bridge)

Below, top to bottom:
Canada geese congregate in the shallows around Indian Pond.

An American bison cools off in the mud by Indian Pond.

This hike takes you past a freshwater wildlife oasis, through quintessential lodgepole pine forest and onto Storm Point, a windswept, wildflower-bejeweled coastal bluff jutting into massive Yellowstone Lake.

Park in one of the two trailhead parking areas just off Highway 14 (on the north side of Yellowstone Lake) about three miles east of Fishing Bridge. Each can hold about a dozen cars. Hike south from the well-marked trailhead past a copse of lodgepole pines and across a grassy plain. Indian Pond sits in an oval basin just to your left. Measuring roughly 1400 feet across at its widest, this watering hole came to be when a crater formed and filled with water after a violent eruption around 3000 years ago. The low ridge on the opposite side of the pond is a remnant of the old crater rim.

In spring and summer, Canada geese frequent the little pond, some even rearing their young along shoreline meadows. They may signal your arrival with some honking as a warning to each

other—and to you. At three feet long and 12 pounds, many of these stately birds migrate to Canada during summer, breeding in far northern latitudes before returning to Greater Yellowstone in fall—look for their trademark "V" flying formation on the wing.

Another animal you may see cooling off in the shoreline mud is the American bison. The grassy plain you're cutting through is a favorite grazing site for these behemoths, one of the iconic Yellowstone species. Males can measure five and a half feet at the shoulder and 11.5 feet nose-to-tail, weighing some 2000 pounds.

If it's summertime, a few will likely be grazing to your right (west), so proceed with caution, if at all. Be especially aware of any bison that might be drinking or splashing at

◄ A small stream connects Indian
Pond and Yellowstone Lake.

▲ Barrow's goldeneyes bob in the
surf of Yellowstone Lake near Storm
Point.

the edge of Indian Pond, which isn't far from the path you are on. No one wants any surprises.

Cross the plain if it doesn't impinge on bisons' personal space, and head for the trees a third of a mile south. Wooly locoweed sprouts pretty violet flowers here in early summer, while Fendler's meadow rue blooms in stringy red veils. Orchard grass, elkweed, spreading phlox, showy sedge, American beachgrass, parsnipflower buckwheat, cow parsnip, and other ruminant delicacies vie for sunlight on this otherwise sagebrush-dominated plain. Deer, elk, and bison aren't the only ones eating at this wildflower buffet: Birds, bees, and butterflies abound, given the easy access to pollen and nectar.

Halfway across, you'll see a trail cut off to the right (west). Ignore it and continue straight—you'll loop back later. After the grassy plain and another small copse of lodgepoles, you'll arrive at a pocket beach on the shores of Yellowstone Lake. Look for the outlet of a small stream just to the east that connects Indian Pond to the lake here at your feet.

You'll likely see ducks massed just offshore, going for a safety-in-numbers strategy when it comes to fending off eagles and hawks, among other predators. Watch for Barrow's goldeneyes floating on the choppy steel-blue water just offshore. Males are black-and-white, while females are dappled brown.

Just because these ducks stick together doesn't mean they will be spared by peregrine falcons on the hunt. One of the fastest of all birds, peregrines leverage their relatively short four-foot wingspans to fly distances at 55 miles per hour, with mid-air dives for avian prey clocked at more than 240 miles per hour.

With a breeding range from the arctic to the tropics, the peregrine is the world's most widespread and adaptable raptor—though it almost didn't make it through a post-WWII period when widespread use of the pesticide DDT wreaked havoc on its population. Rachel Carson first sounded the public alarm about the dangerous effects of DDT on bird species in her landmark 1962 book *Silent Spring*. Many historians consider Carson's book the spark that ignited the modern environmental movement and a raft of federal laws designed to protect and conserve wildlife and landscapes alike. It wasn't until 1972 that the newly formed US Environmental Protection Agency banned DDT in the United States.

Biologists estimate nearly 4000 nesting pairs of peregrine falcons inhabited North America before 1940; by 1975, that number had shrunk to just 324 pairs. An experimental federal reintroduction program in the 1980s helped return these handsome blue-gray and white birds to the region. These days, hundreds of peregrines spend March through October here, mating, nesting, and raising three to five fledglings per couple while gorging themselves on their favorite foods: songbirds and waterfowl. As soon as fall sets in, they vacate to Mexico or points further south until the following spring.

Peregrine falcons were one of the first species classified as endangered by the federal government back in 1969 due to their calamitous decline as a result of DDT exposure. Today, they've rebounded and were taken off the endangered species list in 1999. ▾

When you've had enough of this little beach, continue on the trail as it heads west along a small bluff above the lakeshore, skirting the edge of and eventually entering the lodgepole pine forest. Eventually the trees give way again, and you'll see the rocky headland of Storm Point up ahead.

The terrain out here feels decidedly seaside, with dwarf Douglas fir trees, common juniper bushes, and

scattered patches of wildflowers punctuating the otherwise wide open, windswept dunescape. Silky lupine, with its signature pale purple coloration, carpets various stretches of the sparsely vegetated landscape out here, while bunches of arrowleaf balsamroot, sporting showy yellow blooms, make occasional cameos. Slender cinquefoil, a form of wild rose, blooms into a yellow flower with five floppy elephant's ears for petals. Meanwhile, native wild strawberry fruits in midsummer, providing a welcome kiss of nature's sweetness to whoever (bird, bear, rodent, ruminant, or human) eats it.

This exposed headland takes the brunt of wind and weather off of Yellowstone Lake, a body of water so big it almost seems like the ocean. Yellowstone Lake is the largest high-elevation (7000-plus feet) lake in North America, covering some 139 square miles with a shoreline 141 miles around. The average depth of the lake is 138 feet, and it holds 12 million acre-feet of water. And the wind sure can whip off of the wide, flat expanse of this lake, which measures roughly 20 miles long and 14 miles across. Most years, it is covered by ice from December to May.

How did this great alpine lake form? The massive eruption about 630,000 years ago that formed the Yellowstone caldera laid the groundwork, and a subsequent smaller eruption around 500,000 years ago created a smaller caldera now known as the West Thumb of Yellowstone Lake. But it wasn't until much more recently (in geologic time) that the lakebed as we know it came to be. Receding glaciers ground out weak segments of rhyolite lava to the east and south of the West Thumb caldera at the end of the last ice age 10,000 years ago. This depression soon filled with water, plants, and wildlife, and just like that, Yellowstone Lake was born.

There could hardly be a better view of Yellowstone Lake than perched on the cliff 30 feet above the water's surface at Storm Point, with the oft-blowing winds forcing white-caps onto the rocks below. Looking south straight across the steely blue expanse, you can make out the snow-

clad peaks of Overlook Mountain, Barlow Peak, and Mt. Hancock, over 20 miles away as the eagle flies.

In your near-field vision, a lonely, wind-shorn whitebark pine hangs on atop the nearest ridge, a fitting symbol of the conservation challenges facing biologists at Yellowstone. This keystone tree species of Yellowstone's high elevation ecosystems is in decline at the hands of a disease called white pine blister rust and periodic infestations of mountain pine beetle, a migrating native insect—each compounded by climate change.

From top: These snow-capped peaks certainly seem closer than the 20-plus miles away they are from this spot at Storm Point.

A storm-coiffed whitebark pine hangs on in the rocks of Storm Point.

Enjoy the setting as long as you can, then meander west along the trail for about a quarter mile to a small spit of rocks jutting into the lake.

If you brought a fishing pole (and a fishing license from the National Park Service), try your hand at casting a line. While longnose suckers, longnose daces, redside shiners, and lake chub live down below in the cold, deep waters of the lake, most anglers are hoping for trout.

Consider yourself lucky if you do snag a Yellowstone cutthroat—although you'll have to throw it back—given the fish has been edged out of much of its territory by the larger, more aggressive non-native lake trout. The latter fish, native to Canada, Alaska, the Great Lakes, New England, and parts of Montana (but not Greater Yellowstone) was surreptitiously stocked here, presumably to increase anglers' odds of success, at some point during the early 1990s.

These days, lake trout are the dominant fish species in Yellowstone Lake, despite ongoing efforts by the park service to remove them through managed gillnetting and allowing anglers to take home all the fish they can catch. These large, brown, spotted trout have thrived in their new home

People cast for trout off the rocky spit just west of Storm Point. ▾

▴ A Yellowstone cutthroat trout sports a distinctive red slash under its jawline and medium-sized dark spots along its golden-brown body. The dorsal fin also tends to be spotted, while the underside fins take on a reddish hue.

▴ Lake trout here are bigger than native Yellowstone cutthroats—so much so that the latter make up a large percentage of the former's diet.

because they are the biggest kids on the block, and as such can occupy deeper areas of the lake to escape human predation. They are also at an advantage reproductively here, as they can spawn directly in the lake, unlike their native Yellowstone cutthroat cousins, which must get upstream to reproduce. Native cutthroats comprise a large part of lake trouts' diet, too.

Sadly, these stocked trout have decimated the native Yellowstone cutthroat population in the lake and its tributaries. Data gathered from federally funded creel surveys (aggregate catch reports from recreational anglers) show that prior to 1994, when lake trout were first discovered in Yellowstone Lake, the average landing rate by anglers there was just north of one and a half Yellowstone cutthroats per hour of fishing. By 2006, the average landing rate for the native fish was down to less than half a fish per hour of casting.

Subsequent lake trout suppression efforts have been moderately effective, with the average landing rate for native fish now just below one per hour. Data suggests millions of Yellowstone cutthroats inhabited the lake prior to 1994, while these days there are only tens of thousands of the native fish left. The effect of this takeover reverberates upstream as well, where the number of spawning Yellowstone cutthroats has declined by almost 99 percent in formerly teeming tributaries like Clear Creek.

But a $20 million investment in reducing lake trout numbers in Yellowstone Lake has begun to pay off in recent years with professional fishermen using gillnets from boats equipped with fish-finder technologies to haul in between 200,000 and 300,000 of the non-native encroachers every summer. National Park Service biologists think they can get Yellowstone Lake's population of lake trout down to 100,000 fish or less by 2025 by continuing these removal practices.

Even with these efforts to stymie lake trout, it's unlikely native Yellowstone cutthroats will return to their former abundance, given other pressures. One of the biggies is competition from, predation by, or hybridization with introduced

This Douglas fir has taken to spreading out sideways, instead of growing straight and tall like its peers in the forest, due to its compromised position at the edge of weather-battered Storm Point. ▾

A common raven at Storm Point. ▸

non-native fishes such as rainbow trout, brook trout, and brown trout, none of which live in Yellowstone Lake but now occupy just about every non-thermal waterway throughout Greater Yellowstone alongside cutthroats. Another threat is rising temperatures due to global warming, which heat spawning streams to unacceptable levels. While these iconic fish are on the comeback trail, how far they will get is anybody's guess.

When you've had enough of lake views and fish population dynamics, continue on the trail as it meanders lakeside for another quarter mile before turning north, back into the pines. This mixed-age forest contains lots of downed trees given all the wind that blows off the lake here.

As you hike, you may spot a golden-mantled ground squirrel before it scampers off. Woodpeckers suggest rhythms, and songbirds offer melodies, but that's not why human hikers may be singing. This is prime bear habitat, and you wouldn't want to surprise one as you round a curve in this woodland section of trail; indeed, singing might be the best way to let a bear know you're nearby. Also have your bear spray ready just in case.

In about three quarters of a mile, the trees give way and you're back at the grassy plain. Continue another tenth of a mile and take a left at the junction with the main trail, where you didn't turn earlier, and follow it for a quarter mile back to the trailhead and your vehicle. You'll have learned a lot about some of Yellowstone's most iconic ecosystems on this diverse, delightful hike, and hopefully gotten to see some wildlife, too.

ISA LAKE

While it may look like any other lily pad-covered stillwater pond around the Northern Rockies, Isa Lake here at Craig Pass (elevation 8262 feet) along Highway 191, nine miles east of Old Faithful Village, is truly something special: It's the only known body of water in the United States that drains to both the Pacific and Atlantic oceans. The western end of this 8000 acre, 200-foot-deep lake flows into the Firehole River, which meanders east to the Missouri and Mississippi rivers before draining into the Gulf of Mexico (part of the Atlantic Ocean). The eastern end of Isa Lake empties into nearby Shoshone Lake, which itself drains via a convoluted route into the Lewis, Snake, and Columbia Rivers west to the Pacific.

A small pullout from this stretch of the Grand Loop Road gets you up close and personal with this glorious little bifurcation (or double-draining) lake covered in Indian pond lilies. Isa Lake, sitting as it does above the natal trout streams elsewhere in the park, is a fishless body of water. But plenty of other life frequents the shoreline and surface of this serene alpine lake.

Tucked in among lodgepole pines on all sides, Isa Lake is a peaceful setting and well worth a quick stop along the drive between Old Faithful and Yellowstone Lake.

GEYSER HILL AND OBSERVATION POINT

Famed geyser basin with a less-crowded woodland hike to a perch above it all

DIFFICULTY
Easy to Moderate

LOCATION
Southwest Yellowstone (Old Faithful)

HIKE LENGTH
2 miles

Most of the four million-plus annual visitors to Yellowstone catch an eruption of Old Faithful, the park's symbolic geyser.

You can't come to Yellowstone without seeing Old Faithful, and this short hike not only gets you up close with the world's most famous geyser and the adjacent geothermal basin, it also gives you a thigh-burning climb up to a lookout perch with a commanding view of the pine-dominated, fire-scarred landscape near and far.

Park at Old Faithful Village and find your way to the sidelines of Old Faithful, where you may as well sit or stand and wait for this most famous of the world's geysers to erupt. Indeed, this geyser, with 90- to 120-foot eruptions year-round every 60 to 110 minutes, is a dynamic yet delightfully predictable wonder of nature. The length of each Old Faithful eruption varies from a minute and a half to over four minutes, with shorter eruptions expelling around 3700 gallons of water and longer ones spewing more like 8400 gallons.

A new generation of lodgepole pines has arisen here in the ashes of the 1988 wildfires that ravaged landscapes like this one across Yellowstone. ▾

The National Park Service has constructed elaborate viewing areas around this celebrated geyser that accommodate thousands of visitors at once and usually keep people far enough away that they don't get sprayed by the geyser's 204°F water spout—or 350°F steam. Don't try to get any closer (both for your own protection and for the good of the fragile crust immediately surrounding the geyser).

To avoid the crowds, hit up Old Faithful as early in the morning as you can. Bus tours disgorging thousands of visitors typically come between noon and 6 p.m., so avoid afternoon and early evening if you want more room on the path. Likewise, visiting Yellowstone in spring or fall instead of summer avoids most of the park's four million annual visitors.

Pick a good spot and wait for the next eruption, and try to enjoy the camaraderie of the crowd. Once it does blow, you can judge for yourself whether it was worth waiting for. Old Faithful may not be the highest geyser in the park—that distinction goes to Steamboat Geyser in Norris Geyser Basin, which blows as high as 380 feet at irregular intervals—but it is the most reliable and pretty darn impressive in its own right.

When you've witnessed your requisite blast, follow the paved walkway around to the east side of the Old Faithful viewing area and pick up the marked trail forking to the right (northeast), heading toward Geyser Hill and the other geothermal features of Upper Geyser Basin. Cross the Firehole River on a footbridge, ignoring the turnoff for Observation Point Trail for now, as you'll loop back after Geyser Hill.

For now, continue north as pavement turns to boardwalk over crusts too fragile and unsafe for human footsteps. Multiple signs warn to stay on boardwalks and trails or risk fines, burns, and potentially a painful death.

Ross' bentgrass carpets many of the spaces between geothermal features. This unique herbaceous species grows in vapor-dominated areas such as around geothermal vents, on the walls of hot springs, and on top of geothermal depressions. Clusters of sulphurflower buckwheat, a hardy perennial that blooms in pretty yellow pompoms, make occasional appearances.

Least chipmunks, with reddish-brown bodies and black-and-white racing stripes on their heads and down their backs, dart over rocks and fallen logs, seemingly knowledgeable about where they shouldn't be (that is, on sinter-covered, thermally heated sections of ground). At the other end of the mammalian spectrum, American bison sometimes stray from nearby grazing lands into the Upper Geyser Basin; always give these one-ton ungulates plenty of room and get the heck away if they hold their tails up straight, a sign of an imminent charge.

At a fork in the boardwalk, follow the half-mile Geyser Hill loop counterclockwise (though either way around is fine). You'll pass a variety of geothermal features—Rock Spring, Dome Geyser, Vault Geyser, Teakettle Spring, Pump Geyser, Doublet Pool, Aurum Geyser and Ear Spring—as you round the north side of the loop.

At the next fork in the boardwalk, go straight (south), and in another 200 feet, you'll see Heart Spring and a host of others beyond: Arrowhead Spring, Marmot Cave Geyser, Blowout Geyser, Beehive Geyser, Anemone Geyser, Bronze Spring, and, right before the junction where the loop began, Sulphide Spring. Turn right (south) to retrace your steps back over 200 feet of paved pathway, and head east onto the well-marked Observation Point Trail you passed before.

This dirt trail quickly ducks into a copse of young lodgepole pines and proceeds with minimal elevation gain for about a quarter mile. Evidence of the 1988 wildfires—charred standing dead tree snags, downed lodgepole trunks piled like matchsticks—that tore through this part of Yellowstone with a vengeance is everywhere. While the extent of the damage is amazing to see some three-plus decades on, what's even more incredible is the recovery of the flora across the landscape in such a relatively short time. Thousands of young lodgepole pines have now taken the places of their predecessors along the trail and up the surrounding hillside.

A variety of wildflowers adorn the trailside as well: yellow columbine, spreading dogbane, wild blue flax, and Rocky Mountain penstemon among them. Meanwhile, leathery

◄ Rocky Mountain penstemon (left) and yellow columbine are two wildflowers you'll find here.

creeping barberry fills in the gaps, blooming with showy yellow flowers in spring and fruiting out in spare clusters of grape-like berries in later summer. The berries start pale green and ripen to a purple-blue. This plant's prickly green leaves lose their chlorophyll and turn scarlet red or purple over winter.

Soon enough, the trail begins to gain its 200 feet in elevation via a couple of switchbacks up to the Old Faithful Viewing Area, a point at 7500 feet elevation with a bird's-eye view down into the Upper Geyser Basin and Old Faithful, a third of a mile away as the crow flies. This is a great vantage point to sit and wait for Old Faithful to blow, especially if you saw it up close an hour earlier.

When you've had enough of this astounding panoramic view, retrace your steps to the junction and head east another two tenths of a mile to the parking lot at Old Faithful Village. Including the Geyser Hill detour and the trek up and back to Observation Point, your total hiking distance comes to just shy of two miles.

While the Upper Geyser Basin in general may be the most crowded part of Yellowstone, the throngs are here for a reason. The dynamic nature of the geothermal landscape provides just the kind of escape we can all use from our electronic devices and social media accounts—although no one will stop you from taking a Yellowstone selfie. While you'll be squarely on the beaten path for most of this walk, there aren't many short hikes in the world that offer so much natural eye candy and educational content in such a short span.

BISCUIT BASIN AND MYSTIC FALLS

Geysers and hot springs followed by forested splendor and a dramatic curtain waterfall

LOCATION
Southwest Yellowstone (Old Faithful)

DIFFICULTY
Easy

HIKE LENGTH
2.2 miles

The short trek through Biscuit Basin and onto Mystic Falls highlights some of the best scenic features of Yellowstone National Park, both in terms of thermal activity and forested natural beauty, over a short, relatively level 2.2 miles. While you won't be alone, you will find less of a crowd than at other more famous attractions nearby.

Find the Biscuit Basin parking area and trailhead off Highway 89, two miles north of the Old Faithful Interchange. Follow the boardwalk across the Firehole River, which may be steaming as vapor from the 80°F water mixes with cool air above it. The riverbed is often covered with thick mats of green vegetation that thrive in this thermally warmed, moist, sun-drenched environment. Once you've crossed, crumbly ground dotted with bubbling springs and aqua-tinted waterholes surrounds you in every direction.

Stick to the boardwalks of Biscuit Basin (and other thermal areas of Yellowstone), as the ground may only be a thin crust above boiling hot springs or scalding mud. You can't gauge a safe path by sight, as new hazards can bubble up anytime, anywhere. Heat isn't the only hazard—some of the thermal pools are acidic enough to burn through leather hiking boots. Over the years, more than a dozen visitors have perished at Biscuit Basin after straying from the boardwalk, and hundreds more have been badly burned or scarred. For this reason, the National Park Service prohibits leaving the boardwalk or trail and does not allow pets in thermal areas. Other no-nos include throwing objects into geysers or other thermal features, collecting natural specimens of any kind, and defacing formations—any of which can result in thousands of dollars in fines, bans from entering the park, and even jail time.

Within 200 feet you'll see Black Opal Pool, a crater formed by a 1934 explosion that nowadays breaks down into three distinct red oxide-fringed waterholes; the farther two are tinted a chalky teal, while the closer one retains a greenish hue. The next thermal feature on the right, Wall

‹ Black Opal Pool is one of the first delights you'll encounter visiting Biscuit Basin.

↑ Sapphire Pool looks inviting, but don't even think about it unless you want to risk death by boiling, not to mention a hefty fine and probably jail time if you survived.

◄ Travertine terracing is common throughout Biscuit Basin and the Upper Geyser Basin it lies within, as well as Yellowstone's other thermal areas.

Pool, is more than three times as large as Black Opal and features a similarly chalky teal color.

The fun is just beginning. Note the white-shrouded reddish travertine terracing all around. Travertine is a form of limestone composed of minerals derived from calcium carbonate. Unlike limestones in the ocean composed of the shells of marine organisms, travertine forms when calcite and aragonite precipitate as hot water (in the 77°F to 163°F range) is expelled from the subsurface and solidify into a deposit. As such, you'll see a lot of it around the thermal features of Yellowstone National Park.

In another few steps, you'll encounter mesmerizingly beautiful Sapphire Pool, a thermal feature many consider the highlight of Biscuit Basin. The roughly 50-foot depth and intense heat of this small pool (18 by 30 feet) is responsible for its deep blue hue. The water temperature (159.8°F on average) is too hot to support any kind of microbial life, so Sapphire Pool remains crystal clear.

The aquamarine blue color in the center of this and other thermal pools around Yellowstone is due to the way light waves refract (or bend) as they pass from air into water. The water essentially acts as a prism, breaking down the full spectrum white light from the sun into its constituent colors. Different wavelengths refract at different angles, and the resulting isolated colors travel at different speeds as they pass through the prism. Blue light scatters the most and thus reflects back to our eyes first. We perceive the sky as blue based on the same principles of light refraction.

Biscuit Basin is named for the biscuit-shaped sinter deposits that rimmed Sapphire Pool prior to August 1959, at which point the Hebgen Lake Earthquake reworked the underground plumbing below Yellowstone's central basin. Sapphire Pool became a powerful geyser, with five-minute-long eruptions every two hours that reached heights of 200 feet. While this geysering was an attraction in its own right, the force of the water obliterated the namesake sinter "biscuits" that had rimmed Sapphire Pool. These forceful eruptions lasted another five years, and then the geysering activity gradually slowed, subsiding completely by 1991, when it became the tranquil aquamarine blot we know today.

▲ Common blue-eyed grass attracts pollinators with handsome purple and yellow blooms in early summer.

Looking around, you'll notice scattered bunches of standing dead lodgepole pines with distinctive bobby-socks patterns on their trunks where silica from shifting thermal runoff has intruded into the trees' root systems, killing them from within. Some of them have been toppled by wind or fallen of their own accord, providing dramatic natural framing for otherworldly vistas in every direction.

At the first boardwalk junction, go right to loop around for more views of northern Biscuit Basin. Look for Black Pearl Geyser on the left, a cavernous, steaming hole surrounded by mossy vegetation that thrives around the mineral-laden surface. Superheated water inside is constantly boiling.

Next on the left is Mustard Spring, featuring a small aquamarine center surrounded by a radial band of oozing mustard-yellow goo. This yellow color presents along the edges of many of the thermal springs around Yellowstone, where water temperature is about 165°F, the upper limit for microbial activity. A cyanobacteria called *Synechococcus* thrives in these balmy thermal edge waters, giving them their signature mustard hue.

Avoca Spring, with an average temperature of 193.7°F, bubbles up on your left in another 300 feet. This inkblot sparkles aquamarine in the middle, while rust-colored thermophiles, another warm-water bacteria, cascade off the edges and into the surrounding soils. Avoca Spring features constant churning and overflowing activity but enters sporadic periods of dormancy related to the earthquakes in the area.

At the fork in the boardwalk, follow to the left if you're just interested in Biscuit Basin, passing Silver Globe Cave Geyser and Shell Geyser to the south side, and Jewel Geyser to the north. Then continue straight at the junction to retrace your steps back to the bridge over the Firehole River and the parking lot.

Fork right at Avoca Spring if you want to venture further to Mystic Falls. This spur takes you past pretty blue West Geyser in another 125 feet, then continues southwest before ending at a junction with the Continental Divide Trail. Back on *terra firma* now, turn right (north) on the wide gravel pathway as it bisects a stand of lodgepole pines. Unlike those in neighboring Biscuit Basin, the trees here are thriving, and you'll find shade along the trail's edge.

Imposing rhyolite cliffs frame the view uphill to the north. Clusters of sulphur flower, parsnipflower buckwheat,

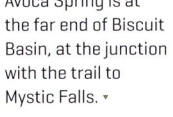

Avoca Spring is at the far end of Biscuit Basin, at the junction with the trail to Mystic Falls. ▾

Clockwise from top left: Creeping barberry, western serviceberry, parsnip-flower buckwheat, lobeleaf, and sulpher flower groundsel are among the showy blooming plants along the trail to Mystic Falls.

lobeleaf groundsel, and western serviceberry jockey for position between the trees, while the sunflowery blooms of arrowleaf balsamroot add an occasional pop of yellow.

Keep hiking and soon enough, you'll parallel the quick, shallow Little Firehole River, steely gray and white in contrast to all the greenery. Soon enough, majestic Mystic Falls comes into view, stair-stepping itself down a series of two major dropoffs for a total fall of 70 feet. It's no wonder how this cascade got its name: wafts of steam emanate from more than a dozen spots up and down its tumbling course. Of the 290-plus documented waterfalls in Yellowstone, this may be the only one over an active thermal hotspot. The misty combination lends the scene an otherworldly aura.

Rumor has it that the negative ions in the air generated by the fast-moving water can lead to feelings of inner peace for those in the midst of the falls. Whether or not you feel the effects, this is certainly a great spot for a break before the next leg of the hike.

If you hear whistling, keep your eyes peeled for yellow-bellied marmots, which frequent the rocky outcrops around the falls. These two-foot golden-brown rodents with short bushy tails are busy during the warmer months, fattening up on the leaves and blossoms of a range of plants before winter. Hibernating in underground burrows, their metabolisms powered down, they enter a coma-like state where body temperature lowers to near freezing, and their hearts beat only four times a minute.

From Mystic Falls, you have two ways back to your car. If you've got some juice left, continue north as the trail climbs some 500 feet over a half-mile and crests the Madison Plateau at the well-marked Biscuit Basin Overlook. You'll get a bird's-eye view of Biscuit Basin, not to mention Old Faithful and the rest of Upper Geyser Basin beyond. Looping this way adds an extra 1.5 miles to the hike and a bit more elevation gain, making it a 3.7-mile excursion.

Otherwise, just retrace your steps back to where you left the boardwalk at the edge of Biscuit Basin (.7 miles), and finish the rest of the boardwalk hike through the basin for a 2.2 mile out-and-back hike.

Either way, you can't go wrong with this less crowded but nevertheless fascinating foray into the wilds of central Yellowstone.

Below, from left: Mystic Falls' 70-foot curtain wall of rhyolite is certainly an impediment to spawning trout, but the Little Firehole River doesn't support much aquatic life anyway due to the superheated thermal inputs along its course.

Lichen-encrusted rhyolite rocks are everywhere on the hike to Mystic Falls.

FIREHOLE LAKE DRIVE

Less-traveled road into the heart of Lower Geyser Basin's thermal features

DIFFICULTY
Easy

LOCATION
West-Central Yellowstone (between Old Faithful and Madison)

DRIVE LENGTH
3.3 miles